SOUTHERN SPAIN

ANDALUSIA · COSTA DEL SOL

Authors:
Gabriel Calvo Lopez-Guerrero
Marion Golder
Mercedes de la Cruz, Elke Homburg
Dr. Sabine Tzschaschel

An Up-to-date travel guide
with 45 color photos
and 9 maps

NELLES

IMPRINT / LEGEND

Dear Reader: Being up-to-date is the main goal of the Nelles series. Our correspondents help keep us abreast of the latest developments in the travel scene, while our cartographers see to it that maps are also kept completely current. However, as the travel world is constantly changing, we cannot guarantee that all the information contained in our books is always valid. Should you come across a discrepancy, please contact us at: Nelles Verlag, Schleissheimer Str. 371 b, 80935 Munich, Germany, tel. (089) 3571940, fax. (089) 35719430, e-mail: Nelles.Verlag@t-online.de

Note: Distances and measurements, including temperatures, used in this guide are metric. For conversion information, please see the *Guidelines* section of this book.

LEGEND

★★ ★★	Main Attraction (on map) (in text)	**Granada**(Town) **Alhambra** (Sight)	Places Highlighted in Yellow Appear in Text			National Border
★ ★	Worth Seeing (on map) (in text	✈ ✈	Int'l, Nat'l Airport			Tollway
						Expressway
❽	Orientation Number in Text and on Map	**Mulhacén** 3478	Mountain (altitude in meters)			Principal Highway
						Main Road
◾	Public or Significant Building	\ 13 /	Distance in Kilometers			Secondary Road
◾	Hotel	☀	Beach		⛴	Ferry
◾	Market	♣	National Park		⊖	Bordercross
✝ ✡ ☼	Church, synagogue	🛈	Tourist Information		⑨⑨⑨	Luxury Hotel Category
⌂	Castle	∴	Ancient site		⑨⑨	Moderate Hotel Category
		⋒	Cave		⑨	Budget Hotel Category
						(for price information see "Accomodation" in Guidelines section)

SOUTHERN SPAIN
Andalusia, Costa del Sol
© Nelles Verlag GmbH, D-80935 München
All rights reserved

First Edition 2000
ISBN 3-88618-720-9 (Nelles Travel Pack)
ISBN 3-88618-782-9 (Nelles Pocket)
Printed in Slovenia

Publisher:	Günter Nelles	**Printing:**	Gorenjski Tisk
Managing Editor:	Berthold Schwarz	**Lithos:**	Priegnitz, Munich
Editor:	Chase Stewart	**Cartography:**	Nelles Verlag GmbH,
Photo Editor:	K. Bärmann-Thümmel		Munich

TABLE OF CONTENTS

HISTORY

TRAVELING THROUGH ANDALUSIA

FEATURES

GUIDELINES

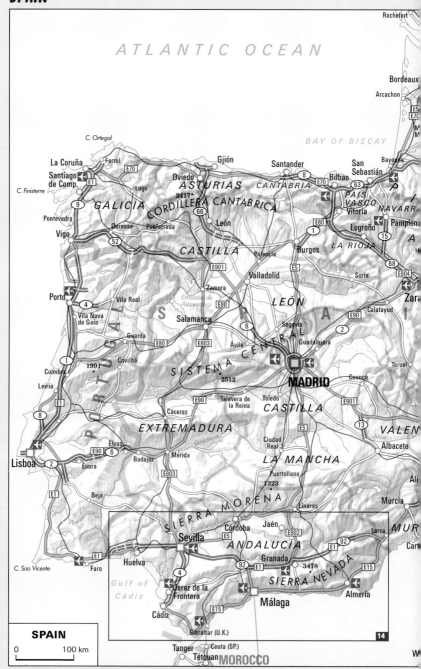

ATLANTIC OCEAN

BAY OF BISCAY

Rochefort

Bordeaux

Arcachon

C. Ortegal

La Coruña
Ferrol
Gijón
Santander
San Sebastián
Bayonne

Santiago de Comp.
C. Finisterre
Lugo
Oviedo
ASTURIAS
CANTABRIA
Bilbao
PAIS VASCO
NAVARRA

GALICIA
CORDILLERA CANTABRICA
2417
León
Vitoria
Logroño
Pamplona

Pontevedra
Ourense
Ponferrada
Palencia
Burgos
LA RIOJA
Soria

Vigo
CASTILLA
Valladolid
Duero
LEÓN
Calatayud
Zar

Porto
Vila Real
Embalse de Almendra
Zamora
Segovia
Guadalajara

Vila Nova de Gaia
Douro
Salamanca
Ávila
MADRID
Cuenca
Teruel

Guarda
SISTEMA CENTRAL
Toledo
CASTILLA

Coimbra
1991
Covilhã
2512
Talavera de la Reina

Leiria
PORTUGAL
Cáceres
EXTREMADURA
Guadiana
Ciudad Real
VALEN

Lisboa
Elvas
Badajoz
Mérida
Albacete

Évora
LA MANCHA
Puertollano
1323
Ali

Beja
SIERRA MORENA
Linares
Murcia

C. Sao Vicente
Faro
Huelva
Córdoba
Jaén
MUR

Gulf of Cádiz
ANDALUCÍA
Granada
3478
Lorca
Car

Jerez de la Frontera
Sevilla
SIERRA NEVADA
Almería

Cádiz
Málaga

Gibraltar (U.K.)

Tanger
Ceuta (SP.)
Tétouan
MOROCCO

6

In the Beginning

Circa 20,000 B.C. The *Cueva de la Pileta* in Andalusia is one of the most impressive testimonials to prehistoric art in Spain.

Circa 2500 B.C. Monumental burial and cultic sites, for example in Antequera, show that Spain was a center of megalithic culture.

Circa 1100 B.C. The Phoenicians erect trading centers along the coast, including what would later become Cádiz and Málaga.

From 600 B.C. The Carthaginians take over the Phoenician and Greek trading centers along the southern and eastern coasts of Spain. They grow into the leading maritime and trading power in the Mediterranean region; a position which would soon be contested by the Romans.

Romans and Visigoths

From 206 B.C. The founding of the first Roman colony, *Itálica*, forms the basis for a deep-reaching Romanization of the Iberian Peninsula. The Roman emperors Trajan, Hadrian and Theodosius come from Spain.

From A.D. 400 Fall of the Roman Empire. The Vandals give their name to Andalusia (Land of the Vandals).

450-711 The Visigoths establish themselves on the Iberian Peninsula and make Toledo the capital of their empire. In 587 they are Christianized under Recared I.

Beneath the Crescent Moon

711 The Berber ruler Tariq Ibn Ziyad conquers the troops of the Visigoth king Roderick in Andalusia. Nearly the entire peninsula falls under Moorish domination.

722 Beginning of the *Reconquista*, the Christian reconquest of the country.

756 The Omayyad Abd ar-Rahman I of Syria founds the independant Emirate of Córdoba.

929 Abd ar-Rahman III elevates Al-Andaluz to the independant Caliphate of the West.

1031 The Caliphate of Córdoba is broken down into numerous constituent kingdoms (*Taifas*).

1085 Conquest of Toledo by the Castilian king Alfonso VI.

1086-1145 The Berber dynasty of the Almoravids establishes itself as ruler of Al-Andaluz.

1150 The Almohads supplant the Almoravids and make Sevilla the center of their empire.

1212 In the Battle of Las Navas de Tolosa the Almohads succumb to Christian troops. King Ferdinand III of Castile then conquers almost all of southern Spain.

1238-1492 The Kingdom of Granada is the last bastion of the Moors.

1469 The marriage of Isabella of Castile to Crown Prince Ferdinand of Aragón creates the basis for the union of the two kingdoms.

Successful rule through personal union: The Catholic Monarchs Isabella...

1478 The Inquisition begins with the systematic persecution of "heretics."

1492 The Kingdom of Granada is taken, ending the centuries-long mission of the *Reconquista*. Isabella I and Ferdinand II are granted the title "Catholic Monarchs" by the Pope. The forced baptism of Jews begins, as does the expulsion of Jews who do not convert, and later the Moors.

1503 Sevilla is awarded a monopoly on trade with the new colonies.

Habsburg Rule

1516 After the death of Ferdinand, his nephew Charles I ascends the throne as the first Habsburg king.

1519 Charles I is crowned German emperor as Charles V.

1556-98 Investiture of Philip II, son of Charles.

1568-70 Rebellions by Moriscos, forcibly converted Moors, in Granada and in the Alpujarras are brutally suppressed.

1609 Philip III expels the last Moriscos.

...and Ferdinand led the Reconquista to its end (anonymous, Prado, Madrid).

Spain under the Bourbons

1701-14 In the War of the Spanish Succession the Bourbon Philip of Anjou prevails over the Habsburg Grand Duke Charles of Austria. Gibraltar is awarded to Great Britain in the Treaty of Utrecht (1713).

1808-14 Napoleon's troops occupy all of Spain with the exception of the port city of Cádiz.

1812 In Cádiz, the *Cortes* (national assembly) adopts the country's first liberal constitution.

1814-33 King Ferdinand VII returns from French imprisonment. He annuls the constitution of 1812 and rules as absolute monarch.

1873-74 The First Spanish Republic does not last long; with Alfonso XII the restoration of Bourbon rule begins.

1889 Spain loses its last colonies with the independence of Cuba, Puerto Rico and the Philippines.

The Twentieth Century

1923 General Primo de Rivera establishes a dictatorship in Spain.

1931 After the victory of the Republicans in communal elections, Primo de Rivera steps down, King Alfonso XIII goes into exile. The Second Republic is formed.

1936-39 A military revolt under General Franco in Spanish Morocco signals the start of the Spanish Civil War, in which half a million people lose their lives.

1939-75 Generalísimo Franco rules with an iron hand; all opposition is suppressed in its infancy. In the Second World War Spain remains largely neutral, which is widely seen as a political success for Franco; in light of the country's terrible economic situation, however, this is a decision based purely on politcal reality.

1975 After Franco's death, King Juan Carlos I ascends the throne, and along with President Adolfo Suárez begins the democratization of Spain.

1977 The first free parliamentary elections since the Civil War are held.

1978 Spain becomes a constitutional monarchy with a parliamentary system of government.

1981 A putsch attempt by the Guardia Civil and the military fails. Juan Carlos I takes a decisive stance in support of Spanish democracy.

1982 Spain joins NATO. The socialist Felipe González is elected President.

1986 Spain is admitted into the European Union.

1992 The *Expo* world exhbition takes place in Sevilla.

1996 José María Aznar wins parliamentary elections as the head of the conservative *Partido Popular*, thereby replacing President González as head of state.

1999 The light athletics world championships are held in Sevilla.

ANDALUSIA

ALMERÍA PROVINCE
GRANADA / MÁLAGA
GIBRALTAR / CÁDIZ PROVINCE
ON THE ROUTE
OF THE WHITE VILLAGES
SEVILLA / HUELVA PROVINCE
CÓRDOBA / JAÉN

Andalusia – Between East and West

Andalusia epitomizes everything that is commonly thought of as "typically" Spanish. The passion of flamenco, the death-defying stance of the proud toreros before an angry bull, the collective pathos of Holy Week, the eternally festive mood under the Andalusian sun – these are the images that come spontaneously to mind in connection with the southernmost region of Spain. And as with many clichés, there is a measure of truth in these images. More bullfighting and flamenco happen in Andalusia than anywhere else on earth, and no other region of Spain holds as many festivals. Yet it would be a mistake to reduce this 87,000-square-kilometer autonomous region encompassing eight provinces, and its approximately seven million inhabitants, to such simplistic notions.

Andalusia is rife with contradictions. Feudal structures still rule the land, dooming all attempts at land reform to failure. The region's large landowners call the shots, while multitudes of day la-

Previous pages: A little señorita in colorful costume – the pride of any Andalusian grandfather. At Whitsun hundreds of thousands of pilgrims visit the Madonna of El Rocío. Left: In the Mezquita of Córdoba.

borers eke out a miserable living by working the fields during the olive and grape harvests. The cities, however, have changed in recent years, and now have a well-established middle class. But urban survival is not an easy matter in Andalusia, which has the highest unemployment rate in Spain. Tourism, especially on the much-maligned but highly popular Costa del Sol, has somewhat made up for this by inducing what appears to be lasting economic growth in the region.

Contrasts also characterize the extreme variety in Andalusia's geography. Almería is the most arid region in all of Europe. Less well known, however, is the fact that inland from the Costa del Sol, in the Sierra de Grazalema, more precipitation falls than in any other region of Spain. The snowy peaks of the Sierra Nevada – a place of Edenic perfection for skiers– lie only a few kilometers from the coast, with its subtropical vegetation.

During the time of Moorish domination, which in southern Spain lasted for nearly 800 years (711-1492), Andalusia was a major player on the stage of world events. The Alhambra in Granada and the Mezquita in Córdoba, as well as the labyrinthine streets of the "white villages," still evoke the presence of the "sons of the desert."

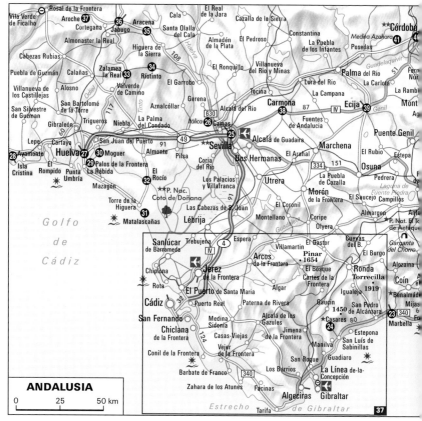

ANDALUSIA

```
0        25        50 km
```

ALMERÍA
Sun-scorched Mountains and Deserted Beaches

In comparison to other provinces in southern Spain, Almería is something of a wallflower when it comes to attracting tourists. Tucked away in the southeast corner of Andalusia, the province lies at a considerable distance from the well-trodden tourist routes of southern Spain. It also lacks the kind of unique sightseeing attractions that draw throngs of visitors to such provinces as Granada, Sevilla and Córdoba. But many appreciators of this region approve: everything in Almería is not yet oriented towards tourism, which means that much almost virgin territory

remains to be discovered. The coastal landscape around the rocky headlands of Cabo de Gata beguiles the visitor with its unspoiled beaches and sleepy fishing villages. Inland is Europe's only desert, a backdrop for the numerous westerns that have been made there, the film industry having long ago discovered its cinematic virtues. And in the midst of the sun-scorched mountains near Tabernas is located one of the largest European experimental stations for solar energy – an ideal location, as it receives Europe's highest number of sun-hours per year.

The west coast, nicknamed the "Plastic Coast," is bizarre in an entirely different sense. Around Campo de Dalías and El Ejido, tomatoes, cucumbers and egg-

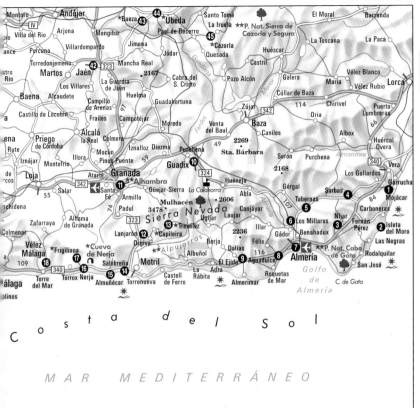

plants ripen in record time under kilometer-long stretches of plastic tunnels. Over the past few decades, several seaside resorts, such as Roquetas de Mar and Aguadulce, have been built – admittedly with somewhat more attention to aesthetics than those on the Costa del Sol, but no one would award them a prize for architectural excellence either.

Cabo de Gata Nature Reserve

The coastal road that runs through eastern Almería is as deserted as it is scenic, with mountains frequently looming over the roadway. The traditional fishing villages of **Garrucha** and **Mojácar** ❶ are now popular seaside resorts, but have sac-

rificed none of their original charm. This is largely because, as they are clustered along the beach, the new hotels and resorts have left the old town center intact. Thirty kilometers south of Mojácar is **Playa de los Muertos**, a beach of silken sand that can be reached by footpaths from Barranco del Horno, gateway to Cabo de Gata Nature Reserve. The road to the cape does not follow the coast, heading inland at Carboneras towards Nijar, from which narrow roads lead into the Cabo de Gata reserve. Between the Cabo de Gata and Sierra de Alhamilla mountains lies the arid plain of Campos de Nijar, which today is covered with the aforementioned plastic tunnels for growing early vegetables.

Isleta del Moro ❷ is a typical fishing village: white houses, beached fishing boats and the public wash-house on the main square. At the opposite end of the bay is Playa de los Escullos with its steep cliffs of white porous rock from which the two rocks of Isleta can be seen. The locals say it resembles a whale and its offspring. In the 16th century, Philip II and his armada sailed away from these shores to do battle with the Turks, taking with them most of the trees in the forests of the Sierra de Cabrera, which were felled to provide wood for the royal fleet.

Following the road out of **Fernán Pérez** to the abandoned village of Higo Seco and the defunct Rodalquilar gold mine takes you to a magnificent sandy beach, **Playa de Rodalquilar**. The coastal areas here are far more densely populated than the interior. Their rocky

Above: Peppers are set out in the hot sun to dry. Right: In the desert of Tabernas stand ghost towns that were sets in Western films made in the 1960s.

beaches notwithstanding, **Las Negras** and **San José** do have some tourist facilities. A boat excursion along the coastline rewards visitors with the discovery of numerous alluring coves that are inaccessible overland.

The best beaches and most scenically satisfying cliffs await discovery between San José and the cape itself. A rather poorly maintained road leads through Playa de Monsul to the "Genoese" beach beyond it, where merchants from Genoa used to load their ships with Moorish silk which had come all the way from Granada by caravan. Footpaths constitute the only access to the deserted coves beyond, which is where the unbelievably bizarre rock formations of **Arrecife de las Sirenas** begin.

★★Sierra de Cabo de Gata Nature Reserve, famous for (volcanic) rock formations of its own, extends over 26,000 hectares. The interior of the park is comprised of a bleak, sweltering hot landscape in which only a few indigenous plants have managed to survive: dwarf palms, cork oaks, wild olives, mastica and prickly pears. Palm groves provide welcome shade in the few oases the park has to offer, but they occur only rarely.

For centuries, human beings have tried to tame this hostile wilderness and its pitilessly intense light. But visitors soon realize that the struggle has been largely given up, and the sight of abandoned farmsteads constitutes a reminder that the area was populous at one time. One of the farmsteads, El Fraile, was the scene of the impassioned episode that inspired García Lorca's folk drama *Boda de Sangre* ("Blood Wedding").

The town of **Nijar ❸**, perched on the slopes of the Sierra de Alhamilla and dominated by a watchtower, is famous for its traditional blue-green pottery and rag mats. The women of the town deftly cut and shape multi-hued odds and ends of fabric into patterns which are then transformed into floor and wall adornments in

local workshops; visitors can watch the craftsmen at work.

Through the Desert

The backlands of Almería contain Europe's only desert, as mountain ranges hem in the region on all sides, depriving it of coastal rainfall.

Sorbas ❹ is picturesquely situated on a table mountain. White houses peek out over the edge, and the cliff is dotted with entrances to cave dwellings. The people of Sorbas make earthenware pottery. The surrounding area contains numerous geological wonders, among them limestone caves, sinkholes and subterranean lakes of awesome beauty. Inasmuch as these sights have not been developed for tourism, adventurous souls should make sure they are appropriately equipped before setting out on an exploratory expedition.

West of **Tabernas ❺** the desert begins in earnest, its core a moonscape extending over 2,200 square kilometers, cleft by deep ravines that turn into powerful masses of moving water following cloudbursts. Although it might seem that no living creature could survive here, the area is nonetheless a unique repository of African flora and fauna – 2,500 endemic plant species in all, some of which explode into magnificent bloom in spring. The reserve also provides a haven in a heartless world for such reptiles as redtailed lizards and adders, for scorpions, and for such avian creatures as kestrels, little owls, barn owls, partridges, warblers and linnets.

At the turnoff to Granada, another small road leads southeast and upwards to the **Colativí**, from which an unforgettable panoramic view of the desert, the Campo de Nijar and the coast can be enjoyed from 1369 meters above sea level.

The terrain and light in this area bear such a close resemblance to that of the Arizona desert that in the 1960s and 1970s the area gave birth to an Old World "Wild West," nicknamed **Mini-Hollywood**. Some of the films made there later became world-famous. The sets were surrealistically left behind, and they now serve as backdrops for stunt shows which are put on for the benefit of tourists. Visitors with a proclivity for things scientific can pay a visit to the largest European experimental station for solar energy, which is right near Tabernas.

Those with an interest in prehistoric times should continue southwards for a stretch and take the turnoff to **Santa Fé de Mondújar**. Near here, at **Los Millares** ❻, the remains of a transitional Neolithic to Bronze Age civilization has been unearthed that existed about 4,700 years ago in Andalusia and the Levant. The excavations indicate that the area now encompassed by the Tabernas desert must have been quite densely populated at one time. The traces of a walled settlement as well as the foundations of round houses, towers and wells are easily discernible, as are the over 100 megalithic graves in the adjacent necropolis.

Almería – Reflection of the Sea

The provincial capital of **Almería** ❼ (population 167,000) is a lively city, and certain parts of it feel more Moroccan than European. The city's name is derived from the Arabic word *al-mariya*, ("reflection of the sea"). Almería's cityscape, which unfortunately also harbors numerous architectural monstrosities, is dominated by the Alcazaba fortress.

For centuries, Almería's harbor has been the backbone of the local economy. Today it is used primarily for the export of fruit, vegetables and flowers grown in greenhouses on the west coast.

Almería enjoys a mild climate year-round, and in summer is the scene of music, flamenco and jazz performances. Local cuisine, encompassing fish, shellfish and other traditional delicacies, awaits discovery in the city's countless bars and restaurants.

Right: View of Almería from the Alcazaba.

Like so many Andalusian cities, Almería was at its height during the period of Moorish domination. In the reign of Abd ar-Rahman III (10th century) it was the most important port and armory in the Caliphate of Córdoba. It then became an independent *taifa* (kingdom), a status it enjoyed for 100 years. The most important legacy of Moorish Almería is the ★**Alcazaba**, the fortress built by Abd ar-Rahman III on a hill overlooking the city. The towers, called the Torres del Homenaje, de la Justicia and de los Espejos, as well as the bastion of Espolón and the remnants of three ring walls provide food for thought about what these fortifications might once have looked like.

The church of **San Juan** was built on the site of the principal mosque, whose prayer niche has been preserved. The church is in the Almedina quarter, which lies between the Alcazaba and the harbor, where an Arab-style tangle of alleys invites exploration.

The Gothic **Cathedral**, which was built in the form of a fortress, once served to protect Almería from raids by Barbary pirates. A stroll through the area around the Cathedral leads either to Bendicho Square, with its intimate atmosphere, or to ancient, arcade-framed **Plaza de la Constitución**, the site of the Town Hall.

Most of the city's daily life unfolds near **Puerta de Purchena**, on Paseo de Almería and Calle des las Tiendas. **La Chanca**, a residential quarter lying between the harbor and the Alcazaba, is all in radiant white and contains rows of small, cubic houses, as well as cave dwellings.

Costa de Almería

The foothills of the Sierra de Gador mountains run down to the sea, making it difficult even today to leave Almería from the west. In summer, 13-kilometer-distant **Aguadulce** ❽ becomes many Almeríans' home away from home, and

young people from throughout the province spend warm summer evenings in the bars and discos at the marina. The coast is lined with holiday *urbanizaciones* (housing) of erratic attractiveness.

Beyond Aguadulce, the mountains pull back somewhat from the shoreline. Before them stretches the **Campo de Dalías**, an area of thick scrubby underbrush that until recently was inhabited exclusively by herds of goats. Ubiquitous here too is the plastic vaulting for vegetables destined for export to the four corners of Europe.

The region is sparsely settled, but its inhabitants have preserved the traditional architecture of the Alpujarras, the region from which they originally emigrated. The heart of this region is **El Ejido ❾**, a town which has experienced a burst of unplanned growth owing to success in the realm of horticulture.

To the south is the resort of **Almerimar**, where tourists can revel in such amenities as hotels, beaches, a marina and a golf course.

GRANADA AND ENVIRONS

Though countless poets have lavished lyric praise upon the city of Granada, no author has surpassed the expressiveness of the words penned by poet Federico García Lorca (1899-1936) about the city of his birth: "Granada is a city of leisure, a city of contemplation and fantasy, a city in which lovers inscribe the name of their beloved in the sand more readily than in any other city… Granada is made for dreams and reveries."

The magic of this place is due in large measure to its North African heritage. Granada reached its greatest splendor as the final stronghold of the Moors under the Nasrid Dynasty (1238-1492). The Alhambra, palace and fortress of the Nasrids, still testifies to the highly evolved architecture and culture that characterized this period.

Nestled between the mountains and the sea, Granada's situation makes it special as well. The ski slopes of the Sierra Nevada are a stone's throw away, as are the

popular recreational area of Las Alpujarras and the earthy charm of Granada's wild, mountainous landscape. The coast of the province of Granada is evocatively named the Costa Tropical and is an area in which tourism has wrought much change. However, unlike the neighboring Costa del Sol, the north coast has for the most part retained its Anadalusian charm.

Guadix – City of Caves

Guadix ⑩, situated ca. 60 kilometers north of Granada, can be easily reached from Almería via the A 92. The town is situated on a rugged plateau in a reddish landscape whose delicate beauty is best appreciated in the waning light of the late afternoon sun.

Guadix is famous for the *Barrio Santiago, a district with cave dwellings in

Above: Granada, the royal city of the Nasrids, with the Alhambra and the Generalife before the magnificent backdrop of the snow-capped Sierra Nevada.

which one-third of the city's 30,000 inhabitants make their homes. Visitors interested in the background to this unusual habitat can visit the **Cueva Museo** (Cave Museum). Perhaps a better bet, though, is to tour one of the actual caves. Many of the cave dwellers are more than happy, for a small fee, to show visitors around their one-of-a-kind habitations. The temperature inside the caves remains constant throughout virtually the entire year. In summer, they provide protection from the heat, in winter likewise from the cold, and running water and electricity are now the norm. Apart from the fact that the occupants of the caves pay no rent, another great advantage of this lifestyle is the virtually infinite expandability of the living space. Some of these caves, ensconced in innumerable hills, are the homes of local potters who produce traditional unglazed earthenware.

The best view of the Barrio Santiago and its white chimneys, which look like outgrowths of the hills themselves, is from the Moorish **Alcazaba** fortress.

Also worth visiting is the **Cathedral**, a handsome structure that was built on the ruins of a mosque.

Perched on a hill south of Guadix is the castle of the margrave, **La Calahorra** (1810), which was commissioned by the nobleman Marqués Rodrigo de Mendoza after he was banished here for instigating an insurrection. To remind himself why he was in Guadix, he had the motto "Not of my own free will" inscribed at the entrance to his abode, the first Renaissance castle in Spain. Built in a mere seven years, the martial austerity of its exterior belies the palatial splendor of the structure's interior.

**Granada –
Royal City of the Nasrids**

The road that leaves Guadix to the west wends its way over the **Puerto de la Mora** pass (highway 342), affording spectacular views of the snowy peaks of the Sierra Nevada. They form a splendid backdrop for the city of **Granada** ⓫, which meanders across a series of gentle hills located in a fertile valley. Rather gloomy suburbs have sprung up around the old town center, and traffic is constant and chaotic: something which all 300,000 Granadinos have been forced to learn to live with. Even the area around the Alhambra has succumbed to this onslaught. Granada, to be truly enjoyed, should be visited outside of the peak tourist season and should be explored on foot; by far the best way to get to know the countless nooks and crannies that make this one of the most beautiful cities in the world. Granada is at its liveliest in the evening, when students put away their books and enjoy the city's innumerable tapas bars and discos.

Granada has a long and interesting history. The city entered a golden age after the fall of the Caliphate of Córdoba in 1031. The Berbers took power, making Granada the center of a *taifa* (small king-

dom). In 1090, Granada fell to the Almoravids, who reunited the fragmented kingdom of Al-Andalus, which was conquered by the Almohads in the 12th century. After the fall of the former capital city of the Caliphate in 1236, the Almohads came under increasing pressure from advancing Christian forces. In 1238, the Nasrid ruler Ibn al Ahmar took advantage of the turmoil and founded the Kingdom of Granada.

From the outset, the Nasrids treated the Castilian royalty like vassals, which allowed the small Kingdom of Granada to survive until 1492. The alliance between the Moors and Castilians was dissolved when Christian factions were united in 1469 by the marriage of Princess Isabella I and the infante Ferdinand II. Spain's campaign against the last Moorish strongholds lasted for over 11 years, until 1492, when Boabdil, the last Nasrid king, handed the keys to the city to the Catholic Monarchs. Like the Jews, the Moors were given a choice between exile and conversion, which resulted in an exodus that had disastrous consequences for Granada's development. The Jews and Moors who chose to stay lived in constant fear of the Inquisition.

The **Alhambra: Pinnacle of Moorish Architecture**

The **Alhambra** ❶, the incomparable royal seat of the Nasrid kingdom, stands on Sabica Hill, with the snow-covered peaks of the Sierra Nevada outlined in the distance creating an imposing natural backdrop for it. In the 13th and 14th centuries, thick walls and numerous fortified towers were built around the palaces that comprised the complex. The fortress proper is called the **Alcazaba**, which was built when the Berbers ruled the land. Its foundation walls are still discernible. From **Torre de la Vela** there is a splendid view of the city. Opposite the tower lies the **Albaicín**, which was originally the

Andalusia

Moorish craftsmen's quarter. Below the Albaicín was the *medina*, which grew up around the mosque. After the city was taken by the Christians, they built the Cathedral on the site of the mosque and extended the city into the floodplain of the Genil River.

Some sections of the Alhambra fell victim to the **Palacio Carlos V**, which Charles V ordered built in 1526. With its elegant courtyard, it is regarded as a jewel of the High Renaissance, although its close proximity to the fanciful filigree architecture of the Alhambra makes it seem somewhat out of place. Today the palace is home to the **Museo Nacional de Arte Hispano-Musulmán** downstairs, and on the upper level, the **Museo Provincial de Bellas Artes**.

The best-preserved palaces in the Alhambra are the **Torre de Comares**, built under Yussuf I (1333-54), and the Patio de los Leones, which was constructed during the reign of his son Mohamed V (1354-91). Beneath the dome of the Torre de Comares, which depicts the Seven Heavenly Kingdoms, the king received ambassadors who entered through the **Patio de los Arrayanes** and were dazzled by the trove of riches they saw there.

The royal apartments were grouped around the **Patio de los Leones**, in the middle of which splashed the famous fountain, with its base comprised of 12 lions. In the courtyard is a veritable forest of arches on delicate columns which treat visitors to an enchanting play of light as they walk beneath them. On either side are halls with impressive star-shaped, ribbed domes. There is a legend that in one of the halls, the *Abencerraje*, a member of the family of the same name was murdered. The other room, the *Sala de los dos Hermanas* (Hall of the Two Sis-

Right: The fountains and gardens of the Generalife make the heat of a summer's day bearable.

ters) is so named because of the two beautiful marble slabs on the floor. Next to this room is the entrance to the *Mirador de Daraxa,* a vantage point from which, owing to buildings that were added by Charles V, today's visitors can "only" look out on the Renaissance courtyard, where the entrance to the Moorish baths is located.

The **★Jardínes del Partal** contains the throne room of Mohamed III, and above it the foundations of the palaces of Mohammed II and Yussuf III. From there, you pass though the gardens with their myrtle, cypress and laurel trees, and their violets and carnations, and walk past the "tower palaces" – **Torre de la Infantas** and **Torre de la Cautiva** – until you come upon the **★★Generalife**, the summer residence of the Nasrid rulers. A leisurely stroll through their lush gardens rewards the visitor with splendid waterworks and lovely vistas that soothe and delight the eye. These gardens, which were originally used by the Moors for the more mundane purpose of growing vegetables, only took on their present romantic form in the early 20th century.

From the ★★Albaicín into the Old Town Center

The **★★Albaicín** is comprised of a gnarled tangle of ancient streets and squares redolent with remembrances of things North African. High walls deter prying eyes, church steeples evoke minarets, and omnipresent walled cisterns recall a time when drinking water wasn't on tap. The many dilapidated buildings also reflect the modest socioeconomic status of this largely working class and student quarter. The Albaicín was declared a UNESCO World Cultural Heritage Site in 1994, and Granadinos hope that at some point funds for an architectural facelift will be forthcoming.

The Albaicín is most easily accessed from **Plaza Nueva** in the lower city. This

square is dominated by the **Chancillería Real ❷**, the former royal chancellery. Behind the Mudéjar church of **Santa Ana** the Darro River emerges, flowing past a small **Bañuelo Árabe ❸** (Arab baths) and the **Casa de Castril ❹**, which houses the **Museo Arqueológico**. If after leaving the museum you're still thirsting for knowledge of exotic lifestyles, you can walk down Calle Cuesta del Chapiz to **Sacromonte**, a gypsy quarter with cave dwellings.

From **Plaza Larga**, the vibrant heart of the upper Albaicín, an archway leads to the church of **San Nicolás ❺** and the observation terrace **★★Mirador San Nicolás**, from which the magical beauty of the panorama of the Alhambra, the Sierra Nevada and the lower city will cause even the most sightseeing-saturated visitor to shout Hallelujah.

To return to the lower city, follow Calle Cuesta de la Alhacaba along the (in places) well-preserved city wall, the **Muralla Árabe**, to the **Torre Monaita**. You then descend the hill to the **Arco**

Elvira ❻, which dates back to the 9th century and was originally Granada's main city gate.

The lower city was built by the Christian conquerors. The Catholic Monarchs, for their part, initiated work on the **★Cathedral ❼** (at the southern end of Gran Via de Colón), but it took 181 years to complete. Thus, while the the plan is Gothic, the main façade (by Alonso Cano) is Baroque.

The desire on the part of the Catholic Monarchs to be buried at the site of their great victory led to the construction, in 1504, of the **★Capilla Real** (Royal Chapel) in Isabelline Gothic style. It contains the marble tombs of Ferdinand and Isabella by the Italian artist Domenico Fancelli, and adjacent to them, the tombs of Joan the Mad (Ferdinand and Isabella's daughter) and Philip the Fair. The retable by Felipe de Bigarn is a true masterpiece of Renaissance art. Another treasure here, on display in the sacristy of the chapel, is constituted by the collection of paintings that once belonged to Isabella.

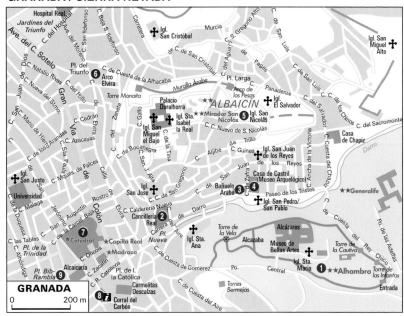

Facing the church is the ***Madraza**, a Koran study center built in the 14th century, from which an extremely moving prayer room has been preserved in the old Town Hall. The building that originally served as the silk bazaar, the **Alcaicería**, was restored in the 19th century following a fire and is now given over to the sale of local crafts.

Across Reyes Católicos street, which runs along the riverbed of the Darros, the visitor comes upon the **Corral de Carbón** ❽, the only Moorish caravanserai in Spain to have survived the ravages of time. On **Plaza de Bib-Rambla** ❾, once the site of tournaments, visitors can relax amongst the flower stalls that have replaced knights in shining armor, and enjoy hot chocolate and *churros* (fritters) in a café.

The Sierra Nevada – Land of Eternal Snow

From Granada, the highest mountain road in Europe makes it way up to the Sierra Nevada (Snowy Mountains) in a southeasterly direction. This range boasts the highest peaks on the Iberian Peninsula, including 19 crests that reach 3,000 meters. The highest of them all is Mulhacén (3,478 meters), followed by Veleta (3,366 meters). From the Veleta Pass, the GR 420 leads into the Alpujarras and to Capileira, although for safety reasons the road is usually closed. This area, which also encompasses the mountainous district of the Alpujarras, was designated a **Parque Natural** (nature reserve) in 1989, and a **Parque Nacional** (national park) in 1998. At first glance, the Sierra strikes the visitor as almost barren. But examined more closely, these mountains turn out to be a botanical treasure trove, with over 2,000 plant species, 64 of which are found only in the Sierra Nevada.

The ski resort of **Pradollanos** is a thorn in the side of environmentalists. Located at an elevation of 2,500 meters and only 36 kilometers from Granada, this nondescript skiing area was transformed into a tourist resort in the 1970s, complete with highrise hotels. For skiers, though, it's heaven on earth, as they can whiz down the slopes under the Andalusian sun from December until the end of May. Even more hotel beds, ski-runs, and ski-lifts have been built since 1996, when the World Skiing Championships were held here.

**Las Alpujarras – The Moors' Last Stronghold

Along the southern edge of the massive Sierra Nevada, parallel to the coastline and extending beyond the confines of Granada and Almería provinces, lies one of the most beautiful mountain landscapes in Spain, the **Alpujarras.

After the fall of Granada in 1492, the Moors withdrew to this remote and rugged mountain landscape. The *Moriscos* (Moors forcibly converted to Christianity) staged numerous insurrections in response to the Christians' failure to comply with the terms of the treaty of surrender they had made with the last Nasrid king, Boabdil. In 1572, Philip II dispatched troops to pacify the region by force and subsequently issued an edict of expulsion requiring all the *Moriscos* to leave the Alpujarras. They were subsequently replaced by Christian settlers from northern Spain.

The flat-roofed, whitewashed houses of the Alpujarras villages still evoke the region's Moorish heritage. In most of these communities, the round of annual festivals includes one called *Moros y Cristianos,* during which the battles between Christians and Moors are reenacted with great fanfare. On terraces that were originally created by the Moors, almonds, fruit and olives are now cultivated. But the income of these mountain farmers is barely enough to make ends meet, and so it is only natural that the younger inhabitants of the Alpujarras emigrate to the cities in order to earn money to support their families. However, now that the region has become a popular recreational and hiking area, young people in the Alpujarras have less of a tendency to leave their native villages.

Orgiva and **Lanjarón** ⑫ are the largest towns in the region. Besides being the western gateway to the Alpujarras, Lanjarón is a spa that has gained renown for its excellent mineral water. Orgiva is where inhabitants of the Apujarras go when they have shopping to do or official business to take care of.

Arguably the most beautiful but also the most frequented area in the region is the **Barranco del Poqueira**, a dramatic gorge that lies at the foot of the highest peaks in the Sierra Nevada. On weekends in particular, visitors descend in droves upon the villages of Pampaneira, Bubión and Capileira in search of both Mother Nature and mother's cooking, the latter in the form of robust Alpujarras specialties.

*Pampaneira, the lowest-lying village in the region, features a lovely church as well as an array of shops selling patchwork rugs, pottery and woolen blankets. Several years ago, in the airy heights of the region, a Buddhist study center opened on the opposite side of the Barrancos. Called **La Atalaya**, it was consecrated in person by the 14th Dalai Lama. In 1985, Ösel Hita Torres, who is revered as the reincarnation of the Lama Thuben Yeshe, was born in Pampaneira, and Tibetans look to him with great hope for the future.

Visitors to *Bubión will discover an admirable and charming resort called **Villa Túristica de Bubión**. Situated on the heights above the town center, it constitutes a departure from the touristic norm in that, architecturally speaking, it is a replica of a typical Alpujarras village.

Since it lies at the fairly vertiginous height of 1,436 meters, *Capileira is a good place from which to take in the surrounding craggy mountain scenery. The

town is also home to a small ethnological museum containing lively and informative exhibits about the history of the Alpujarras. Visitors who would like to achieve even greater (mountain) heights have come to the right place: Pico de la Veleta, at a lofty 3,398 meters the second-highest peak in the Sierra Nevada, can be climbed from here.

★Trevélez ⓭, the highest village in Spain, boasts a crisp, dry climate that is perfect for curing the type of ham called *jamón serrano* that is a specialty of the region. The hams are air-cured for over a year after being pickled in brine.

Yegen stands out on the literary map of Alpujarras. The British writer Gerald Brenan lived in the village for a time, and in the 1950s published an interesting book about the region called *South of Granada*, in which he describes the people of the Alpujarras as being friendly

Above: Mountain-biker on a springtime trip in the Solynieve skiing area (Sierra Nevada, 2,000-2,600 meters above sea level).

and endearing – and so they have remained to this day.

Costa Tropical – The Coast of Granada

The pleasantly imaged appellation of the Granadan coast stems from the favorable microclimate that, thanks to the protection from ill-winds afforded by the Sierra Nevada, prevails in and around Motril, Salobreña and Almuñécar. The good weather also aids and abets the cultivation of avocados, medlars, kakis (Japanese persimmons), mangos, cherimoyas and sugar cane.

The area is relatively calm in comparison with the brouhaha prevalent on the nearby Costa del Sol. Most vacationers encountered on the Costa Tropical come from no farther away than Granada.

Lovely **Salobreña** ⓮ is right on the coast, ensconced atop a sheer cliff that drops straight down to the beach. An active and healthy way to experience this village is to climb the narrow streets lined

Andalusia

with sparklingly white houses to the Arab fortress from which the panorama encompasses the entire coast, the plane below with its sugar cane plantations and, on a clear day, the peaks of the Sierra Nevada. At the foot of the fortress lies the parish church of Nuestra Señora del Rosario with its superb tiled Mudéjar portal. For a snack after all that walking, head towards the Town Hall, from which a stairway leads up to the market. From there, it's only a few minutes' walk to the broad gravel beach, which is also accessible by car.

In **Almuñécar ⑮** the mountains also descend to the shoreline. The town has recently become of the most popular seaside resorts on the coast of Granada, with hordes of hotels and vacation apartments right on the beach. The charming old town is situated on a hill where 2,800 years ago the Phoenicians founded the settlement of *Sexi*. Archaeological digs have uncovered two Phoenician necropolises and an enormous Roman pickling factory, and the archaeological museum has an extensive selection of artifacts from both the Phoenician and Roman periods. At the edge of town, almost hidden from view by tall trees, a seven-kilometer-long Roman aqueduct is still carrying water, just as it did two millennia ago.

Apart from the fishing harbor and a marina, **Motril** doesn't have much to offer. The town is situated in the valley of the Guadalfeo River, where primarily sugar cane is cultivated, a crop that the Moors brought here centuries ago.

MÁLAGA
Sunny Coast and Mountainous Hinterland

The Costa del Sol, Málaga's sun-drenched coast, is one of the most popular holiday destinations in Europe, an annual rendezvous with the pleasures of the seashore for countless vacationers. Paradoxically, neither the poor image that many

have of this region nor the negative criticism evoked by its innumerable architectural eyesores have dented its popularity with the vacationing masses. The temperate coastal climate, characterized by 300 sunny days per year, the long sandy beaches and the subtropical fauna are their own best PR. Visitors who like resorts with lots of action can choose from any of a number of inexpensive package holiday venues in Torremolinos or Fuengirola. Marbella is an entirely different story, however. Here, only the well-heeled need apply – particularly golfers, for whom the red carpet is rolled out. Jet-setters are in their element here, and real celebrities can be glimpsed taking their constitutionals on the promenade down by the yacht harbor in Puerto Banús.

By contrast, the mountainous hinterland of Málaga is worlds away – still relatively peaceful and calm. Mysterious dolmens and an exotic landscape full of evocatively rocky protuberances await visitors to pretty Antequera. The mountain villages of Axarquia, which are easily reached from the seaside resorts of Nerjo or Torre del Mar, are known primarily for their wine and their *pasas*, raisins made from sweet wine grapes. The heart of the region, though, is the provincial capital of Málaga, where much has been done in recent years to give this somewhat dilapidated-looking city a facelift.

Costa del Sol – East of Málaga

The most well-known seaside resort on this stretch of coast is **Nerja ⑯**. Just above the neighboring village of Maro is the much frequented ★**Cueva de Nerja**, a dripstone cave with craggily weird formations. Visitors are only allowed to explore the initial 400 meters, although the cave complex is five-fold longer. The artifacts on display attest to the fact that the cave was inhabited even in Paleolithic times. During the summer, the Cueva de

Nerja is the breathtaking setting for a ballet and music festival.

Along with its maze of tiny streets and whitewashed houses, Nerja has retained much of its atmosphere of ancientness. A broad promenade ends at Balcón de Europa, a good place from which to contemplate not only the sea and the coast, but also the **Sierra de Almijara**, which juts far out into the sea.

*Frigiliana ⑰ is one of the most appealing villages in the Sierra Nevada. Its highest section, the **Barrio Alto**, is quintessentially picturesque, with practically wall-to-wall flowers lining its narrow, hilly streets. The village is surrounded by olive groves and vineyards, the latter produce the succulently dry and sweet wines of Axarquia.

Torrox is ensconced in a valley which opens out towards the coast, ending in wide beaches. Archaeological excavations have uncovered remains of a Roman necropolis and a fish-pickling factory.

The modern-looking seaside resort of **Torre del Mar** (Tower of the Sea) lies at the heart of Araxia, but aesthetically doesn't live up to its evocative name. It is, however, on the way to inland-lying **Vélez-Málaga ⑱**, which in addition to its **Alcázar**, is endowed with some upliftingly lovely churches. The village of **San Juan Bautista** harbors some marvelous *pasos* (procession figures) by Pedro de Mena, as well as **Nuestra Señora de la Encarnación**, an early Christian church which in an earlier incarnation was a mosque.

The Provincial Capital of Málaga – Dynamo of the South

Málaga ⑲, which began life as a Phoenician settlement, counts as one of Spain's most important seaports and, with over 500,000 inhabitants, is the second largest city in Andalusia. Though the sights in this provincial capital don't rival those of Granada, Sevilla or Córdoba, a

visit is certainly not a waste of good holiday time. Málaga has an effervescent atmosphere all of its own, and, what's more, gives visitors a feel for the "real" Spain, as it is largely untouched by the ravages of tourism.

The quickest way to get to know Malagueños in their natural habitat is to head for the ***Mercado ①** on Calle Atarazanas. Once upon a time a Moorish shipyard, it is now populated by purveyors of lovingly erected pyramids of such regional delights as succulent oranges and lemons, intense loquats, exotic cherimoyas and aromatic avocados.

The Renaissance ***Cathedral ②** lies at the center of the Old Town. Built (on the site of a former mosque) in 1528 to commemorate the victory of Emperor Charles V, the locals tenderly term it "La Manquita" (The Deficient One) owing to the church's lack of a second tower, planned but never built. Not to be missed in the soothing interior are Pedro de Mena's gracefully carved choir stalls.

Adjacent to the cathedral lies the small parish church of **Iglesia del Sagrario** (1487), which sports an intricately decorated late-Gothic portal as well as an elaborate Renaissance retable. Opposite the Cathedral, the former episcopal palace now serves as the **Museo Diocesano ③**. A few steps away lies the very heart of Málaga's Old Town, **Plaza de Chinitas**, where there are so many taverns and tiny old-fashioned shops it's hard to know which to enter first. The **Palacio de Buenavista ④** on Calle San Augustín once harbored the Museo de Bellas Artes, but will soon be reborn as the **Museo Picasso**. This most famous of Pablos is a Málagan native son, having spent his earliest years at 15 Plaza de la Merced, only a palette's throw away from the museum and now home to the **Fundación Picasso**.

Calle Alcazabilla deposits you at the front door of Málaga's collective memory lane, the **Alcazaba ⑤**, a fortress whose gargantuan outer proportions recall the

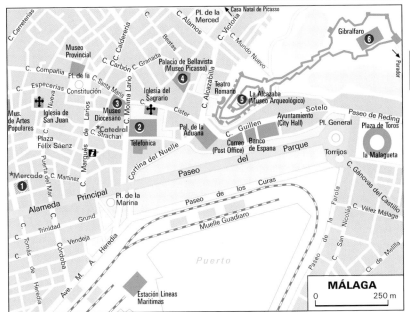

time when the city was the most important seaport and trading center in the Moorish Nasrid Dynasty. The interior is only a shadow of its former self, a point poignantly made by the omnipresent profusion of bougainvillea, roses and jasmine. An aerobically challenging climb to the **Museo Arqueológico** on the highest observation point repays the effort with an inspiring vista of the rooftops and port of Málaga.

High above the Alcazaba rises yet another fortress, the **Gibralfaro** ⑥, which dates back to the 13th and 14th centuries. There's superb strolling and views to be had on the structure's restored outer walls, from which the city and the mountainous landscape beyond evoke well-deserved superlatives. The café at the nearby *parador* is a relaxing place for postcard writing and coffee sipping.

Below this hill of many fortresses, urban life continues on Málaga's most attractive street, **Paseo del Parque**, with such typically venerable constructions as the Customs House and Town Hall.

To experience a more intimate side of the city, visit **El Palo**, the fishermen's quarter to the east of the Paseo, with its low houses and man-made beaches, as well as innumerable *merenderos*, small restaurants serving primarily seafood.

Excursions in Málaga Province

About 50 kilometers north of Málaga on the fertile plateau of the Guadalhorce River lies *★**Antequera**, whose origins stretch back to the Bronze Age. This is attested to by the *★**Conjunto Dolmenico** on the edge of town, comprised of **Cueva de Menga**, **de Viera** and **del Romeral**. These chambers hidden inside man-made hills are believed to have been cultic and burial sites. The largest dolmen, consisting of stones weighing as much as 180 tons, is 25 meters in length. The complexity of this structure suggests that a highly developed urban culture must have flourished here about 4,300 years ago. Neolithic groups in search of minerals ventured forth from what is now Almería,

traversing the entire Iberian Peninsula and eventually making their way to the British Isles. Thus, the name given to the city by the Romans, *Anticaria* (The Old One), from which the modern name is derived, turns out to have been right on target. All that remains of the Moorish **Alcazaba** on **Cerro de San Cristóbal** is its outer walls and keep, as well as a tower in which munitions were stored. Within the fortifications themselves is the fine Renaissance church of **Santa María**, now used for concerts and exhibitions. The vista from here is of a calm sea of white houses, punctuated only by the monastery and church. In the far distance looms the peculiar outline of **Peña de los Enamorados** (Lovers' Rock), so named because legend has it that a Christian and a Moor who had transgressed by falling in love across religious boundaries jumped to their deaths from it rather than

Above: Mijas, an attractive traditional village, offers a magnificent view of the coast. Right: Enjoying the sun on the beach of Marbella.

live without each other. On the way back to the center of town, a detour to a former conventual church of the Carmelite order, **Nuestra Señora del Carmen**, is worthwhile for the manifold Baroque treasures on view within. After passing the church of **San Sebastián**, with its striking and profusely ornamented Baroque tower, you arrive at Plaza del Coso Viejo. Here, in an 18th century nobleman's palace, the **Palacio de Nájera**, the **Museo Municipal** (Municipal Museum) is housed. Its main attraction is the Ephebe of Antequera (1 A.D.), an immaculately executed statue of a Roman youth.

Ten kilometers to the south, the ***El Torcal de Antequera** ⑳ nature reserve, with its 17 square kilometers of pristine nature, provides visitors with a refreshing rest from sightseeing at a refreshing 1,000 meters above sea level. A clearly-marked path, which takes about 45 minutes to traverse, requires good hiking boots. The path meanders through a fairy-tale landscape of rock slabs piled on top of each other like stacks of pancakes,

amongst which a trove of plants and animals thrive. Scientifically-minded visitors will appreciate the attractively simplified scale model of the area's complex geology on display in the **Nature Reserve Information Center**.

Another splendor of nature lies northwest of Antequera near the sleepy village of Fuente Piedra: the 1,300-hectare **Laguna de Fuente de Piedra**, the largest body of salt water in Andalusia, and after the Camargue in southern France the earthly breeding paradise flamingos most frequently flock to. In 1983, the Laguna was declared a *reserva integral* (fully protected nature reserve). To safeguard the fragile ecosystem and give the flamingos some privacy, the lake was fenced off. But during the breeding season (March to July) the narrow road that goes around the lake provides excellent opportunities to find out everything you ever wanted to know about flamingo mating behavior.

South of Laguna de Fuente is another nature reserve called **Ardales**. Over the millennia, the Guadalhorce River carved its way to the sea, thereby creating a gorge called **Garganta del Chorro**. A footpath for the adventurous follows the gorge 200 meters up. Visitors averse to strolling along a potentially lethal precipice should opt instead for a walk along one of Ardales' four lovely reservoirs.

Costa del Sol – West of Málaga

The western portion of the Costa del Sol can be accurately described as one gargantuan tourist resort spread along more than 100 kilometers of coastline from Málaga to Estepona. The center of the hubbub lies between **Torremolinos** and **Fuengirola**, with rows of hotels, vacation resorts, amusement parks, stores and restaurants. A gem on the Costa del Sol, ★**Benalmádena** ㉑ provides a welcome relief from all this, with its magnificent floral displays expressing local residents' civic pride, and the **Museo Arqueológico**, which houses intriguing works of art from pre-Columbian sites throughout Latin America.

Neighboring **Mijas** ㉒ is famous for the donkey-drawn taxis that lend the town a distinctive atmosphere. The Virgen de la Peña, said to have appeared to herdsmen here, occupies a grotto where multitudes of votive pictures and candles are left in gratitude for her help. Despite the effects of mass tourism, Mijas and likeminded towns have managed to preserve their architectural heritage. The town's rectangular bullfighting arena shares a hill with several observation points from which the views of the coast can take your breath away.

The star of the show on Costa del Sol is without doubt **Marbella** ㉓, where seeing and being seen is practically an official city religion. Ever since the day in 1959 when Alfonso von Hohenlohe opened his Marbella Club and began throwing his legendary bashes, Marbella has been the darling of the international jet-set, whose crazy quilt of currencies finances the ongoing construction of new hotels and golf courses that appear out of nowhere like pop-up pictures in children's books. In the 1970s affluent citizens of Arabic countries began arriving in such large numbers that jokes began to surface about a second *Conquista* of Marbella by petrodollars. Visitors interested in dancing to the beat of the richest of the rich need only take a walk along the promenade next to the yacht harbor in **Puerto Banús**. Once you've had your fill of stars and starlets (both would-be and authentic), you can resurface to the real world via Plaza de los Naranjos, nearby which a fcw well-tended lanes still evoke the fishing village this town once was.

A fine outing option is the mountain village of *★**Casares*** ㉔ on a rise crowned by an Arab fortress, which can be reached from **San Luís de Sabinillas**. Time marches here to the rhythm of an Andalusia of yesteryear. Hopefully this serene village will resist, at least for a time, the temptation to sign on the Faustian dotted line of mass tourism.

ALMERÍA

ℹ️ Parque Nicolás Salmeron, tel. 950274355.
🛏️ 😊😊 **Guitart Club Alborán**, Alquián Retamar, tel. 950207200, fax 950207010. **La Perla**, Pl. del Carmen 7, tel. 950238877, fax 950275816.
🏛️ **Alcazaba**, daily 10 am-2 pm and 5:30-8 pm (in winter 9:30 am-1:30 pm and 3-6 pm). **Cathedral**, daily 10:30 am-12 pm and 5:30-6:30 pm. **Estación Experimental de Energía Solar**, Mon-Fri 9 am-noon, reservations tel. 950387900. **Cooperativa Artesana de la Aguja** (ceramics), C/ Lope de Vega 7.

GRANADA PROVINCE
ALPUJARRAS
🛏️ 😊😊 **Villa Turística del Poqueira**, Bubión, tel. 958763111, fax 958763136, lovely resort hotel built in the style of an Alpujarras village with good restaurants serving authentic regional cuisine. **Hotel Taray**, Carretera Tabalate-Albuñol, km 18.5, Orgiva, tel. 958784525, fax 958784531, walking paths and horseback-riding facilities. **Miramar**, Av. Andalucía 10, Lanjarón, tel. 958770161, fax 958770161.

FUENTE VAQUEROS
🏛️ **Casa Museo de García Lorca**, Tue-Sun 10 am-1 pm and 6-8 pm (in winter 4-6 pm).

GRANADA
ℹ️ **Corral de Carbón**, C/ de Libreros, 2, tel. 95822-5990 and Plaza de Mariana Pineda 10, tel. 958226688.
🛏️ 😊😊😊 **Parador San Francisco**, Real de la Alhambra, s/n, tel. 958221440, fax 958222264. This luxury hotel has only a small number of rooms, so it's advisable to make a reservation well in advance. **Alhambra Palace**, Peña Partida 2, tel. 958222268, fax 958226404, famous hotel with an oriental ambience. **Saray**, Tierno Galván 4, tel. 958130009, fax 952129161, modern, comfortable 4-star establishment. 😊😊 **Hotel Reina Cristina**, C/ Tablas 4, tel. 958253211, fax 958255728, centrally located hotel where the Granadan poet Federico García Lorca often socialized with a poet friend who lived here. **Gran Vía Granada**, Portigo de Velutti 2, tel. 958285464, fax 958285591, modern hotel. 😊 **Hotel América**, Real de la Alhambra 53, tel. 958227471, fax 9582227470, small, romantic place. **Hotel Niza**, C/ Navas 16, tel. 958225430, fax 958225427, in the center of town.
❌ **Mirador de Morayma**, C/ Pianista García Carillo 2, a wonderful restaurant in the Albaicín with a superb view of the Alhambra. **Restaurante Cunini**, C/

Pescadería 9, a little-known but great place for seafood. **Restaurante Salvador**, C/ Duende 16, rustic restaurant serving classic Granadan cuisine. **Bodega Castañeda**, C/ Elvira 5, popular tapas bar.

🏛 **Alhambra and Generalife**, Mon-Sat 9 am-8 pm, Sun 9 am-6 pm; also Tue, Thu and Sat 10 pm-midnight. Tickets with the day and time of your visit can be purchased in advance at the Alhambra, or you can order them by fax at 958210584. **Museo de Bellas Artes** and **Museo Hispano-Musulman, Palacio Carlos V, Alhambra**, Mon-Fri 10 am-2 pm. **Cathedral**, Mon-Sat 10:30 am-1:30 pm and 4-7 pm, Sun and holidays 4-7 pm. **Capilla Real**, Mon-Sat 10:30-1 pm and 4-7 pm, Sun and holidays 11 am-1 pm. **Cartuja**, Mon-Fri 10 am-1 pm and 4-8 pm, Sun 10 am-12 pm, holidays 10 am-1 pm. **Iglesia de San Jerónimo**, Mon-Fri 10:30-1 pm and 4-7 pm. **Carmen de los Martires**, daily 10 am-2 pm and 5-7 pm. **Museo Arqueológico**, Wed-Sat 9 am-8 pm, Tue 3-8 pm, Sun and holidays 9 am-3 pm.

GUADIX

🛏 🌕🌕 **Mulhacén**, Avda. Buenos Aires 41, tel. 958660750, fax 958660661.
🏛 **Cathedral**, Mon-Sat 10:30 am-1 pm and 5-7 pm, Sun 10:30 am-2 pm.

LA CALAHORRA

🏛 **Castillo**, Wed 10 am-1 pm and 4-6 pm.

SIERRA NEVADA

🛏 🌕🌕🌕 **Maribel**, Balcón de Pradollano, tel. 958480400, fax 95480458. 🌕🌕 **El Lodge**, Balcón de Pradollano, tel. 958480 600.

MÁLAGA PROVINCE

ANTEQUERA

ℹ Palacio de Nájera, Coso Viejo, tel. 952704051.
🛏 🌕🌕🌕 **Parador de Antequera**, C/ García del Olmo, s/n, tel. 952840261, fax 952841312, sensibly modern parador surrounded by lush vegetation, with a swimming pool.
❌ **La Espuela**, Paseo María Cristina, s/n. Pl. de Toros, a restaurant under the seats of the bullfighting arena serving classic regional cuisine.
🏛 **Cuevas de Menga y Viera** and **del Romeral** (dolmen), Mon-Sat 9:30 am-1:30 pm and 3-6 pm, Sun 10 am-2:30 pm.

MÁLAGA

ℹ C/ Chinitas 4, tel. 952213445.
🛏 🌕🌕🌕 **Parador Gibralfaro**, Castillo del Gibralfaro, tel. 952221902, fax 952221904, comfortable parador

with a view of Málaga and the Mediterranean. **Hotel Larios**, C/ Marqués de Larios 2, tel. 952222200, fax 95222240, friendly atmosphere, in the shopping district. 🌕🌕 **Hotel Don Curro**, C/ Sancha de Lara 7, tel. 952227200, fax 95222407, traditional hotel.
❌ **Restaurante Antonio Martín**, Plaza la Malagueta, best seafood restaurant in the city. *TAPAS:* **El Boquerón de Plata**, C/ Bolsa 8 and C/ M. García 11.
🏛 **Cathedral**, daily 10 am-1 pm and 4-7 pm. **Museo de Arte y Tradiciones Populares**, Pasillo de Sta. Isabel 10, Tue-Sat 10 am-1 pm and 4-7 pm, Sun 10 am-1 pm. **Museo de Cofradías**, in Iglesia y Hospital de San Julián. **Alcazaba** with **Museo Arqueológico** and **Ceramics Museum**, Tue-Fri 9:30-1:30 pm and 5-8 pm, Sat 10 am-1 pm, Sun 10 am-2 pm. **Casa Picasso**, Pl. de la Merced, daily 10 am-2 pm.

MARBELLA

ℹ C/ Miguel Cano 1, tel. 95277242.
🛏 🌕🌕🌕 **Marbella Club**, Boulevard Principe Alfonso de Hohenlohe, tel. 952822211, fax 952829884. Marbella owes its status as a gathering place for high society to the hotel's founder, Prince Alfonso von Hohenlohe. Any self-respecting millionaire rents a villa here, and never mind the price. **El Fuerte**, Av. El Fuerte, s/n, tel. 952861500, fax 952824411, a proficiently managed establishment with direct access to the sea. **Tryp Marbella-Dinamar**, Ca. Cádiz, km 175, tel. 95280500, fax 952812346, sports hotel. 🌕🌕 **Club Pinomar I**, Crta. Cádiz km 189, tel. 952831345, fax 952833948, tennis and miniature golf.

MIJAS

🛏 🌕🌕🌕 **Byblos Andaluz**, Urb. Mijas-Golf, tel. 952473050, fax 952476783, has its own golf course. 🌕🌕 **Hotel Mijas**, Urb. Tamisa 2, tel. 95248 5800, fax 952485825, cozy place, restaurant has a superb view of the shoreline, which is about 15 minutes away by car.

NERJA

ℹ Puerta del Mar 4, tel. 952521531.
🛏 🌕🌕🌕 **Parador de Nerja**, Almuñecar 8, tel. 9525 20050, fax 952521997, in a lovely setting. 🌕🌕 **Balcón de Europa**, P. Balcón de Europa 1, tel. 952520800, fax 952524490, many rooms have a view of the ocean. **Casamaro**, Carmen 2, tel. 952529690, fax 952529552, apartment hotel in the village of Maro.
🏛 **Cuevas de Nerja**, daily 10:30 am-2 pm and 3:30-6 pm.

TORREMOLINOS

🛏 🌕🌕 **Hotel Tropicana**, Tropico 6, tel. 952386600, fax 952380568, relatively small seaside hotel (86 rooms), quite comfortable.

*GIBRALTAR

The Rock at Land's End

*Gibraltar ❶ – 6.5 square kilometers of solid rock, and long a bone of contention between Britain and Spain – rises 450 imposing meters out of the sea.

To the annoyance of the Spanish, this strategically crucial cliff has been in British hands since the 18th century. Following a referendum held in 1967 in which 95 percent of Gibraltar's residents voted to maintain their close ties to Britain, Spain abruptly closed its border with the colony and did not reopen it until 1985.

Gibraltar was regarded in antiquity as one of the two pillars of heaven (along with Jebel Musa in Morocco) built by Hercules at the edge of the known world. The name Gibraltar is derived from that of the Berber general Tarik, who in 711 used Gibraltar as a staging point from which to launch his conquest of Spain. The name evolved from Jebel al Tarik, "The Mountain of Tarik."

A road leads from **La Línea** in Spain across an isthmus to the border, right behind which lies an airport runway that travelers must cross over in order to reach the center of Gibraltar City, where the 32,000 inhabitants of this peninsula live. The population is a mixture of people of British, Spanish, Indian and Moroccan origin who communicate with each other in English, Spanish or an unusual-sounding fusion of the two languages called *Llanito*.

Main Street is the province of the duty-free shops. The changing of the guard at **The Convent**, the governor's palace, is British to the hilt, as are the bobbies directing traffic and the fish and chips shops. Outside town there are of course the cliffs, which can be investi-

gated in one's own car, by taxi or via cable car. For a price, a company called **Rock Tours** takes visitors to kitchily-lit **St. Michael's Cave**, a dripstone cave where traces of prehistoric settlements have been found. Above ground and also worth visiting is the 14th-century **Moorish Castle**, which grew out of the ruins of an 8th-century construction.

Those longing to be underground again can head for the **Great Siege Tunnels**. Built during the "Great Siege" of 1779-83, this extensive network of tunnels bristles with embrasures. But of course the principal attraction on Gibraltar is the **Apes' Den**, where the tailless Barbary apes romp about. About the "Gib," as the inhabitants affectionately call their home, it is said: As long as the cute and audacious apes live on Gibraltar, the rock will remain British.

Opposite Gibraltar, on the west side of the **Bahía de Algeciras**, lies **Algeciras** ❷, with its famous harbor for the ferries that every year haul millions of passengers back and forth between Ceuta and Tangier.

CÁDIZ PROVINCE

The fine silken sands of the *Costa de la Luz*, the "Coast of Light" – so named because of the intensity of the sun on the Atlantic coast – extend from the mouth of the Guadiana River to the Strait of Gibraltar. The picturesque fishing villages along the coast feature small hotels and resorts. Here, the commotion prevailing on the Costa del Sol is noticeable for its absence, probably because of the levanto, a dry wind out of Africa that sweeps huge clouds of sand across beaches and through village streets. When it blows, the unspoiled natural surroundings of the mountainous interior offer an enticing alternative – a region comfortably dotted with whitewashed villages and grazing cows. The levanto, while perhaps an ill wind for many tourists, is a blessing for

Right: A surfer traversing the Strait of Gibraltar with Jebel Musa (Morocco) in the background.

surfers, who have made the small town of Tarifa at the southern tip of Spain their mecca.

A major commercial and shipping center that is buffeted by the Atlantic, Cádiz is a city whose praises have been much sung by travelers. Not yet entirely spiffed up for the tourist trade, Cádiz possesses a distinctive charm. At its height (like the rest of this region) during the Age of Exploration, Cádiz developed into a cosmopolitan city with an affluent middle class comprised primarily of merchants. Meanwhile, the rest of Andalusia clung to feudal structures and remained centuries behind, which parts of it still are today. Traditionally, there is rivalry between Cádiz and Jerez, an inland center of sherry production where "sherry barons" still call the shots.

Apart from the wine industry, the breeding of thoroughbred Andalusian horses, as well as bulls for bullfighting, is important to the local economy. Along with the port cities of Puerto de Santa María and Sanlúcar de Barrameda, Jerez is part of the "Sherry Triangle," where various fine brandies as well as world-famous sherries are produced.

The Costa de la Luz

Where the Atlantic and the Mediterranean meet, and only 14 kilometers from Africa, **Tarifa** ❸ is also the gateway to the Costa de la Luz. Beyond the streets of Gibraltar, the fabulous Atlas Mountains, clearly visible in good weather, tempt travelers to hop a ferry from Tarifa to Tangier.

The "high wind area" around Tarifa constitutes the Promised Land for windsurfers. For 300 days of the year the powerful levanto stirs up the atmosphere, resulting in an average daily wind speed of 4.5 on the Beaufort scale, enough to challenge the abilities of even the most experienced wave-riders.

Like most cities and towns along this stretch of coast, Tarifa was founded as a trading outpost by the Phoenicians. Owing to its strategic location, posses-

sion of the town was hotly contested by the Moors during the conquest of the Iberian Peninsula. Alonso Pérez de Guzmán, commander of the **Castillo** at the time, stood firm even after the Moors took his son hostage, threatening to slit his throat. In the end, the heroic father selflessly threw his own sword down to the Moors, thereby sacrificing his son for the Fatherland. For this brave deed the Crown conferred upon him the byname El Bueno (The Good), awarded him extensive lands, and granted him the title Duke of Medina Sidonia.

Northwest of Tarifa, on the beautiful sands of ★**Bolonia** ❹, lie the remnants of the Roman city of *Baelo Claudia* (2 B.C.). Apart from baths, temples and the forum, a fish factory has also been excavated. In the latter, fish pickled in large vats were turned into *garum*, a fish paste in great demand as a condiment throughout the Roman Empire.

Above: Tarifa, the southernmost point on the Iberian Peninsula.

For many villages, **Zahara de los Atunes** ❺ and neighboring **Barbate** among them, catching fish is still the most important source of income. The sanguinary spectacle of the *Almadraba* (tuna fishing) unfolds annually during the months of May and June. The tuna are driven into nets and – in accordance with a tradition stretching back centuries – the fishermen then harpoon their captives to death one by one. Most of the catch is then sold to Japanese wholesalers.

The incomparable beaches at **Caños de Meca** were discovered ages ago by beachcombers, many of whom have moved up in the world and now own very successful small hotels and restaurants. At low tide, caves that give forth fresh water can be explored along the steep coast. **Cape Trafalgar** is indelibly associated with the famous sea battle that took place here on October 21, 1805, during which Admiral Nelson was killed as his fleet triumphed over the French-Spanish alliance, thereby reinforcing England's position as dominant naval power in the

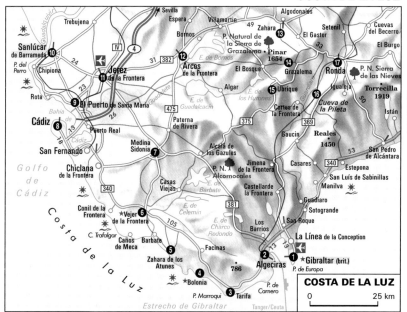

Mediterranean. The fine sand beaches of the charming resort and fishing village of **Conil** extend from the lighthouse at Cape Trafalgar to the village itself, which even during the height of the tourist season is hardly ever crowded.

Set back a few kilometers from the sea, **★Vejer de la Frontera ❻** has retained the character of the Arab town it once was. Extending over several hills, it is reminiscent of the Moroccan city of Chechaouèn, perhaps because both cities were founded in the 11th century by Almohads. Narrow alleys are lined with tranquil, white-washed, almost windowless houses. Family life centers around patios, which are traditionally arrayed with flowers.

Situated inland and surrounded by pastures on which bulls raised for bull-fighting await their fate, **Medina Sidonia ❼** not only bears a poetic name but also has a long history that began, as so much else in this region, with the Phoenicians. The town's past is also tightly bound up with the powerful Medina Sidonia family, which traces its lineage back to the coura-

geous Guzmán el Bueno. For centuries, this aristocratic family's wealth has been derived from extensive land holdings. Plaza Mayor, the church of Santa María Coronada, and the remnants of a fortress complex testify to the town's bygone days of grandeur.

★Cádiz – Siren of the Sea

Among the many compliments poets have seen fit to bestow upon **★Cádiz ❽**, perhaps none is more fitting than José María Pemán's succinct phrase "Señorita del Mar, Novia del Aire" (Mistress of the sea, beloved of the wind). Entwined by the Atlantic in a kind of lover's embrace, Cádiz is linked to the mainland by a narrow, nine-kilometer-long spit of land. A fresh sea breeze keeps the climate inviting during the scorching summer months, although it also gnaws away at the peeling façades of the buildings in the Old Town. Cádiz, squeezed onto a limestone rock with a surface area of less than 20 square kilometers, is starved for space. It has tried to resolve this dilemma with a nightmare of nondescript concrete residential and factory buildings arrayed along a four-lane access road that runs right past the old city gate, the **Puerta de la Tierra**. Fortunately, the beguiling 18th-century Old Town quickly erases the first negative impressions with its narrow and twisting lanes leading to charming squares. The elegantly gleaming whitewashed homes built by Spanish and Italian merchants with cash to spare from hefty trading profits are the stuff of dreams. Some of the most beguiling examples can be seen at **Plaza de San Antonio**: enclosed glass balconies grace façades, and rooftops are crowned with small lookout towers (*miradores*) from which telescope-wielding merchants could watch ships come and go in the harbor. For the past few years, the municipal government has been carrying out extensive renovation, at great expense, in such working-class neighborhoods as **Barrio del Popúlo**.

During carnival in Cádiz the streets are full to overflowing with boisterous *Gaditanos*. Even Generalísimo Franco himself, who tried to forbid carnival celebrations, couldn't stop this event, in preparation for which carnival associations hold meetings all year long where they organize parades, make costumes and compose satirical songs called *chirigotas*. The only carnival in Spain that is at all comparable to Cádiz' is the one in the Canary Islands.

Cádiz has a long and eventful history marked by both dark and glorious moments. The city was founded by the Phoenicians in 1100 B.C. as a trading outpost, making it the oldest continually inhabited city in Europe. The town was originally named Gadir, meaning fortress. Trade flourished under the Romans, who exported silver, copper, wine, wool and

Right: Storm clouds over the Old Town of Cádiz.

salted fish back to Italy. The *Puellai gaditanae*, Cádiz' desirable dancing girls, provided banqueting Romans with postprandial entertainment. But in the 6th century A.D. Roman domination was brought to an end by the Visigoths, who were supplanted by the Moors in 711. About a hundred years later, the Normans invaded and almost completely destroyed Cádiz.

Things only began to look up again in 1260, when Alfonso X ("The Wise") of Castile recaptured the city for the Christians. With the discovery of America, a sustained period of prosperity began. Many a conquistador set out on an expedition from Cádiz, which soon became the second most important seaport on the Atlantic coast, after Sevilla.

Unfortunately, this did not escape the attention of privateers: In 1587, the "Queen's Pirate," Sir Francis Drake, destroyed the Spanish fleet as it lay at anchor in Cádiz harbor. Nine years later, the English Earl of Essex pillaged and laid waste the city itself. However, in 1717 after the Guadalquivir River silted up, Sevilla was forced to cede to Cádiz its trade monopoly with the new colonies, and as a result trade flourished in this liberally-oriented cosmopolitan port city as never before.

During the period in which Napoleon's forces occupied Spain (1808-1814) Cádiz was the only city the French were unable to take. In 1812, the *Cortes* (national assembly) gathered in the free city of Cádiz and adopted Spain's first liberal constitution, which provided for the establishment of a constitutional monarchy. But when King Ferdinand VII returned from exile and took over the reins of power, he at once declared this progressive document null and void.

At the end of the 19th century, Spain lost the last of her overseas colonies, and Cádiz was soon little more than a shadow of its former self. In the 1930s, however, the construction of a free port initiated a

Andalusia

new business upswing. The population of Cádiz is presently 158,000. Major employers include the shipyards, the navy, commercial fishing concerns and the canning industry.

The best starting point for a walking tour of Cádiz is **Plaza de San Juan de Dios ❶**, with its neoclassical Town Hall. North of the plaza is the harbor, the departure point for boats to the Canary Islands. After passing the Town Hall and following **Calle Pelota**, you soon come to the **Catedral Nueva ❷**, which was constructed in the 18th century according to the same ground plan as the Cathedral of Granada.

The Cathedral's stunning gold-tiled dome gives the imposing structure a positively Oriental character. Striking as well is the use to which various building materials have been put in the main façade: the church was begun in marble, but when money ran short, construction continued in less costly limestone. Among the truly superb sights in the Cathedral interior are the Baroque choir stalls, which were orig-

inally in a Carthusian monastery in Sevilla. The crypt contains the tomb of the composer Manuel de Falla (1876-1946), Cádiz' most illustrious native son. Among the church's notable treasures are several striking monstrances, one of which, the **Custodia del Millón** (1721), is adorned with sparkling precious gems. Next door to the Cathedral stands its predecessor, the 17th-century church of **Santa Cruz** (Catedral Vieja).

Cádiz has a long tradition of flower sellers singing the praises of their wares at the market on the small **Plaza de Topete ❸**. The stands around the market hall are almost seamlessy joined to one another. It is well worth taking a peek inside, if only to appreciate the selection of seafood on offer – squid, octopus, swordfish, devilfish, tuna fish and just about every other edible denizen of the Atlantic is represented.

To the north of Plaza de Topete, visitors who enjoy heights can climb to the top of the **Torre Tavira ❹** for a bird's-eye view of the city.

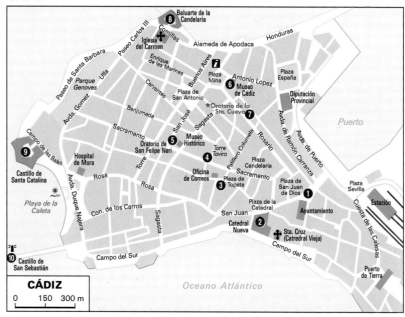

CÁDIZ
0   150   300 m

A memorial plaque on the **Oratorio de San Felipe de Neri ❺** on **Calle Santa Inés** serves as a reminder that in this church Spain's first liberal constitution was passed in 1812, having been inspired by the spirit of the French Revolution.

The next venue of interest can be reached by walking across **Plaza de San Antonio**, with its representative townhouses, to **Plaza de la Mina**, one of the most beguiling squares in Cádiz. Located right on the square is the **Museo de Cádiz ❻**, where the emphasis is on archaeology, painting and folk art. Among the treasures worth seeking out in the archaeology section are two marble sarcophagi (5th century B.C.) that were excavated from a Phoenician necropolis. In the painting section, a cycle of works by Francisco Zurbarán that were originally painted for the Carthusian monastery in Jerez should definitely not be missed. Notable as well is a depiction of the stigmatization of St. Francis by Zurbarán's contemporary, Murillo, who painted this picture for the Capuchin monastery in

Cádiz. While working on another painting in the monastery, Murillo fell from a scaffolding and later died as a result of his injuries. The round chapel of the ★**Oratorio de la Santa Cueva ❼** on **Calle Rosario** (a shopping street) is adorned with three religious paintings by Goya. This church also inspired Joseph Haydn to compose a mass for Good Friday called *The Seven Last Words of Our Redeemer on the Cross.*

After visiting the church, you might want to grab a bite to eat at one of the superb seafood restaurants on Calle Rosario or snack on scrumptious almond pastries at one of the many cafés nearby. Visitors can then work off the caloric consequences on the **shoreline promenade**, the nicest section of which is the **Alameda de Apodaca**. It boasts exuberantly exotic plants, extremely pretty and cozy squares with tiled benches and a series of gorgeous views of the Bay of Cádiz. At the end of the promenade is the **Baluarte de la Candelaria ❽**, a bastion situated opposite the Baroque **Iglesia del**

Carmen. Continuing on to the next section of the promenade the visitor comes upon **Parque Genovés**, a lovely park beyond which there is yet another fortress, the star-shaped **Castillo de Santa Catalina** ❾ and, just in front of it, **Castillo de San Sebastián**. And there's even a beach (albeit a small one) thrown in for good measure – **Playa de la Caleta** with its picture-postcard rows of brightly-painted fishing boats. Almost anywhere visitors walk in Cádiz they feel the unique island-like charm of this delightful city on a peninsula.

The Sherry Triangle

The famous "Sherry Triangle" is comprised of Jerez, the port city of Puerto de Santa María and Sanlúcar de Barrameda. This wine-growing region, whose products are marked with designation of origin labels, encompasses 26,000 hectares. The first grapes were planted here by Phoenicians over 3,000 years ago. As the English could not pronounce "Jerez," over time the name for the fortified wine was anglicized to "sherry." The wine is stored in huge single-story structures (*bodegas*) in which the oak vats containing the sherry are stacked in pyramids. The *solera* process is an ingenious wine-blending technique. The more mature wines are kept on the lowest of the (usually) five tiers of each pyramid. Only one-third of the contents of these mature wines are bottled each year. The wine removed is replaced with wine from the upper tiers of vats, until the uppermost tier begins this process all over again. Then vats with young wines are filled to capacity, after which they mature in the solera for at least five years. This labor-intensive system ensures uniform quality.

Sherry is shipped to the four corners of the earth from **El Puerto de Santa María** ❾, the port city located at the mouth of the Guadalete River. And in the bodegas of this city, smooth Anadalusian brandy is, like sherry, aged by means of the *solera* process.

During the summer months the 70,000 inhabitants of El Puerto de Santa María are joined by innumerable devotees of the town's superb beaches. The mostly Spanish vacationers also appreciate the excellent local seafood specialties served in El Puerto's restaurants.

During the Age of Exploration, rich merchants called the shots here. Christopher Columbus and his helmsman lived for a time in the **Castillo de San Marcos** (13th century), which belongs to the Dukes of Medinaceli. Sights worth visiting here are the church of **Iglesia Mayor**, which Alfonso X ordered built in the 13th century after taking the town; and the **Plaza de Toros**, Spain's third-largest bullfighting arena. The great poet and native son of El Puerto, Rafael Alberti, lived to see the founding of a small museum devoted to his life and work.

Sanlúcar de Barrameda ❿, the second most important city in the Sherry Triangle, is located at the mouth of the Guadalquivir River. This historic commercial center and fishing port is best known as the home of *manzanilla*, a wine whose flavor resembles that of a dry sherry called *fino*. It's said that the damp and salty air of Sanlúcar endow manzanilla with its distinctive flavor. In the upper city, the ruins of the once formidable **Castillo de Santiago** still stand watch over the harbor from which Columbus departed on his third voyage to the New World in 1498. The Portuguese explorer Ferdinand Magellan also set sail from Sanlúcar in 1519 on his ill-fated attempt to circumnavigate the globe. **Nuestra Señora de la O** (14th century) is notable for its Mudéjar-style portal and Rennaissance wooden ceiling. A few steps away is another more modest construction, the palace of the Dukes of Medina Sidonia.

The lower city, which is virtually enveloped by the sea, has lovely squares, churches and Baroque monasteries. On

Andalusia

the edge of town lies the fishing quarter of **Bajo de Guia**, with innumerable bars serving lobster and *manzanilla* wine. As these venues look out on the beach, visitors can contemplate the sea as they enjoy their repast and, when they've finished eating, decide whether or not to take a boat trip to neighboring **Coto de Doñana National Park**, which is not only the largest in Spain, but probably the one most worth visiting for its wealth of African fauna, including lynxes, imperial eagles, flamingos and purple gallinules.

It's almost a duty, when in the sherry metropolis of **Jerez de la Frontera ⓫**, to pay one's respects to at least one of the countless "wine cathedrals," as the *bodegas* are affectionately called here. Many horse aficionados associate Jerez with the **Real Escuela Andaluz del Arte Ecuestre** (Royal Riding School), where every Thursday straight-backed riders on noble Andalusian steeds put their skills to the test. An important equestrian event in Jerez is the elaborate *Feria del Caballo* in May, a horse show for which caballeros and their señoras don flamenco costumes. And for a different but no less exciting event, visitors can join the international clientele at the *Circuito de Jerez* for a fast-paced car race.

With a population of 180,000, Jerez counts as both the largest city in the province of Cadíz and its economic linchpin – a fact poignantly brought home by the surreal contrast between the grand villas of the sherry barons and the miserable farmworkers' districts just outside of town. Old Jerez is relatively small and easy to find one's way around in. Its trademark is the 11th-century **Alcázar**, which contains the remnants of Moorish baths and a chapel, formerly a mosque. The city's most striking ecclesiastical structure is the collegiate church of **San Salvador** (1695), into which are inte-

grated the remnants of buttresses from an earlier Baroque church that constitute an almost dissonant stylistic element. Every year on the church steps, the *Fiesta de la Vendimia* (grape harvest festival) is opened with the benediction of the new wine. The venerable **Plaza Asunción** is the site of two buildings of interest: a handsome Renaissance palace that once served as town hall, and the church of **San Dionisio**, which is consecrated to the patron saint of Jerez. Another site of note is the **Museo de los Relojes**, with a collection of 300 clocks that chime in unison every day at noon. The whys and wherefores of flamenco, an integral part of Jerez' heritage, are documented at the **Museo de Flamenco**.

Situated in front of the old city gates is Jerez' Carthusian monastery, **La Cartuja**, where the renowned portraits of monks by Zurbarán were painted. They now hang in the Museum of the City of Cádiz. Carthusian horses also originated here, the result of cross-breeding dating back to the 16th century. Only men are allowed to visit (by appointment) the interesting Late-Gothic monastery.

ON THE ROUTE OF THE WHITE VILLAGES

In the mountainous interior of the southern tip of Andalusia, in an area demarcated by the cities of Cádiz, Ronda and Tarifa, lie the ****Pueblos Blancos**. Many of these villages have *de la Frontera* appended to their names, which originally indicated that they lay along the Christian-Moorish border, and which today distinguishes them from other *pueblos blancos* of southern Spain. Large areas of Andalusia were already in Christian hands by the 13th century. But it was only 200 years later that the last Moorish stronghold, the Kingdom of Granada, surrendered. Over the course of these two centuries, the towns on the border between Moorish- and Christian-controlled

Right: Riding through a field of sunflowers near Arcos de la Frontera.

territory were repeatedly overrun by the forces of both sides. The inhabitants tried to protect their villages by building fortresses and defensive walls. But these settlements were most effectively defended by the remote, breathtaking mountain landscapes or precipitous escarpments surrounding them.

The region's gleaming dice-like houses receive a new coat of whitewash each year from the women of the village, a tradition that harks back to the Moors. This is also the origin of the expression *pueblos blancos*, or "white villages". The houses harbor romantic flower-bedecked inner courtyards. Their white walls and red roofs, combined with the vibrant green of the surrounding landscape, are enough to make almost anyone want to take up landscape painting. Daily life is tranquil. Centuries of isolation, the effects of which are still palpable, have only recently begun to yield to the inexorable demand for tourist amenities. Some villages now offer excellent accommodations for foreign guests in the

form of small hotels and pensions. Tourism has also helped to stem the flood of young people migrating from the villages to the big cities.

Situated on a high rock, **★Arcos de la Frontera ⑫** is one of the most beautiful of the white villages. For cars and pedestrians alike it's a long, steep climb up the narrow main street to **Plaza del Cabildo**, where a café in the parador provides refreshment. A lookout point on the plaza is downright vertiginous, with a wall of rock dropping 160 meters straight down to the Guadalete River. The square contains the Gothic church of **Santa María de la Asunción** and its gleaming, richly-ornamented Isabelline west portal. The church, which has been rebuilt numerous times, is somewhat ungainly when viewed from outside, which makes the elegance of the palm wood vaults inside all the more startling. The Baroque choir stalls were carved by the great Andalusian sculptor Pedro Roldán.

A walk through serpentine streets past former monasteries and palaces of noble-

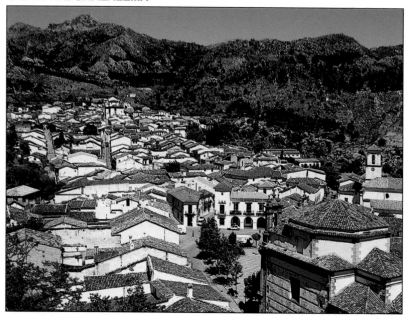

men leads to the parish church of **San Pedro**, which is built in a variety of historical styles.

The Sierra de Grazalema

Beyond Arcos, where the Guadalete River has been dammed to make two large lakes, the road begins climbing to the most beautiful of the white villages: El Bosque, Benamahoma, Ubrique, Grazalema, Ronda, Setenil, Olvera, Zahara and Jimena de la Frontera. They are all watched over by the Sierra de Grazalema, which is part of the Serranía de Ronda range. The highest peak, **Pico de Torreón**, reaches to 1,654 meters.

In 1984, a 47,000-hectare area was designated the **Parque Natural de la Sierra de Grazalema**, Andalusia's first nature reserve. Many people are amazed to learn that more rain falls here than anywhere

Above: Grazalema, one of the "white villages," is the jumping-off point for a trip into the Sierra de Grazalema National Park.

else in Spain, mostly in spring and winter. It originates in masses of clouds blowing in from the Atlantic and has the greatest impact on the limestone mountains, where over the centuries a rugged and dramatic landscape of countless caves, cliffs and ravines has been carved out. The fauna of the Sierra is just as variegated, the most common tree species being holm oak, cork oak, carob and wild olive. In spring, the scent of wild herbs is in the air, among them rockrose and rare species of orchid. The most fascinating botanical pearls here are the pinsapo pines, a holdover from the Tertiary period. The **pinsapo forest** in the **Sierra del Pinar** is located north of the road between Benamahoma and Grazalema. Information about paying the forest a visit (permitted only with a park guide) is available from the park offices in Grazalema and **El Bosque**. The landscape in the park provides an ideal refuge for many species of birds of prey, and in recent years the Iberian ibex have been making a comeback. Ideally suited as a

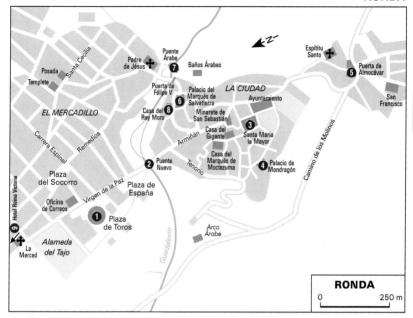

jumping-off point for exploring the park are the lovely white villages of **Zahara de la Sierra ⑬** and **Grazalema ⑭**. If the weather is uncooperative, an alternative is to pay a visit to the weaving workshop in Grazalema where attractive hand-woven blankets and ponchos can be purchased. Visitors interested in acquiring fine leather goods should consider visiting **Ubrique ⑮**, also home town of the famous bullfighter Jesulín de Ubrique. The dripstone caves of **Cueva de la Pileta ⑯** near Benaoján contain prehistoric drawings of animals.

**RONDA
The Birthplace of Bullfighting**

****Ronda ⑰** (pop. 30,000), perched impregnably on a mountain, is divided into an old and new town by the 160-meter-deep gorge (*tajo*) of the Guadalevín River, which has been spanned since the 18th century by a remarkably constructed bridge. This appealing town with its old arena steeped in tradition attracts hordes of day-trippers from the only 50-kilometer-distant Costa del Sol. The onslaught only subsides in late afternoon, gradually giving way to tranquility.

Ronda's antiquity has been amply documented by prehistoric finds, as well as by excavations of Roman settlements and Arab baths. A good place to begin a walking tour is at Spain's oldest bullfighting arena, the **Plaza de Toros ①**, which dates from 1785. The bullfighting tradition in Ronda is inextricably bound up with the Romero torero dynasty. In 1720, Francisco Romero became the first bullfighter to go "eye to eye" with a bull. His uncle, Pedro Romero, established the rules for modern bullfighting, which call for the bullfighter to be on his feet rather than mounted on horseback as was originally the practice. The small **Museo Taurino** contains garments worn by famous toreros, stuffed bulls' heads, and posters and photographs from past bullfights. Nowadays, bullfights are usually held in Ronda in September only, during the *Feria de Pedro Romero*. In honor of this great tore-

ro, the bullfights are conducted in historic costume. Spectators pay astronomical sums for a seat in the arena, which has a capacity of only 5,000.

The **Puente Nuevo ❷** (New Bridge) spans the Tajo River in the Old Town. **Santa María Mayor ❸**, Ronda's most interesting church, is located on Plaza de la Duquesa de Parcent. The church was built after the Reconquest in 1485 on the remnants of a mosque, whose minaret was crowned with a belfry. In the vestibule of the church, an exposed arch from a *mihrab* (prayer niche) in the former mosque attests to the magnificent Islamic house of worship that once stood here. The church is divided into two distinct sections – the west side, which dates back to the Gothic period, and the east side, which was rebuilt in Renaissance style following an earthquake. The most impressive sculpture in the church is a Dolorosa by the sculptress Luisa Roldán. Near

Above: Ronda – in a spectacular setting at the edge of the Tajo gorge.

the church is the **Palacio de Mondragón ❹**. Originally the palace of the taifa kings, it contains enchanting terraces, Renaissance frescoes and Arab tilework. The main thoroughfare of the Old Town leads to the mighty city gate, the **Puerta de Almocávar ❺**, just in front of which stands the single-nave Gothic church of **Espíritu Santo**, which the Catholic Monarchs ordered built in the 15th century following the Reconquest.

Back in the center of town, before you reach the Puente Nuevo, a steeply inclined street on the right leads down to the 18th-century **Palacio del Marqués de Salvatierra ❻**. A Plateresque portal ornamented with unusual sculptures leads into this spacious, sumptuously furnished palace. The gardens open out onto a marvelous view of the Serranía de las Nieves, from which the Guadalevín River and the **Puente Árabe ❼** (Arab Bridge) that spans it can be seen. Also in the valley below are the **Baños Árabes** (Arab Baths), testimony to the technological sophistication of the Moors. A lovely footpath on the right bank leads past beautiful gardens to the commercial center of town, en route to which the visitors' eye will be caught by the **Casa del Rey Moro ❽** (House of the Moorish King). Legend has it that Christians imprisoned here were forced to fill amphoras with water from an underground spring and then carry the containers up 300 steps.

Devotees of the poet Rainer Maria Rilke should not miss the opportunity to visit the venerable **Hotel Reina Victoria ❾** in the newer part of town. In room 208 there is a small museum in Rilke's honor. A bronze statue in the garden reminds visitors that the poet spent the winter of 1912-13 in Ronda.

About 12 kilometers northwest of Ronda are the vestiges of **Ronda la Vieja**, the original Ronda founded by the Romans, where the ruins of a theater and amphitheater are among the most interesting sights.

CÁDIZ PROVINCE

ARCOS DE LA FRONTERA

i C/ Belén, tel. 956702264.

▣ ⊕⊕⊕ Parador Casa del Corregidor, Pl. España, tel. 956700500, fax 956701116.

⊕⊕ Marqués de Torresoto, C/ M. de Torresoto 4, tel. 956700717, a small, charming hotel.

CÁDIZ

i C/ Calderón de la Barca 1, tel. 956211313.

▣ ⊕⊕⊕ Parador Atlántico, Duque de Nájera 9, tel. 956226905, fax 956214582, comfortable and modern parador in the northwest corner of the old town, near Parque Genovés. **⊕ Imares**, C/ San Francisco 9, tel. 956 212257, nostalgically old-fashioned, but clean.

✕ Restaurante El Faro, C/ San Felíx 15, specializes in seafood dishes, prices on the steep side.

🏛 Museo de Bellas Artes and **Museo Arqueológico**, Tue-Sun 9:30 am-2 pm. **Museo Historico Municipal**, Tue-Fri 9 am-1 pm and 4-7 pm, Sat/Sun 9 am-1 pm. **Oratorio de San Felipe Neri**, daily 8:30-10 am and 7:30-10 pm. **Cathedral**, Mon-Sat 11 am-1 pm. **Cathedral Museum**, Tue-Sat 10 am-1 pm. **Oratorio de la Santa Cueva**, Mon-Fri 10 am-1 pm. **Tavira Lookout Tower**, C/ Marqués del Real Tesoro 10, daily 10 am-8:30 pm (in winter 10 am-6 pm).

EL BOSQUE

🏛 Cuevas de la Pileta, dripstone caves, Benaoján, daily 9 am-2 pm and 4-7 pm.

🏃 Information center for **Parque Natural Sierra de Grazalema, tel. 956727029 (an advance reservation is required for some hiking paths).

JEREZ

i Alameda Cristina 7, tel. 956331150.

▣ ⊕⊕⊕ Hotel Guadalete, Av. Duque de Abrantes 50, tel. 956185478, fax 956182293, a comfortable and modern establishment.

⊕⊕ Torres, C/ Arcos 29, tel. 956323400.

⊕ Nuevo Hostal, C/ Caballeros 23, tel. 956331600.

🏛 Museo de los Relojes "La Atalaya," C/ Cervantes, Mon-Sat 10 am-2 pm. **La Cartuja** monastery, Tue-Sun 4-6 pm (only men are allowed to visit). **Alcázar** and **mosque**, Mon-Fri 10 am-2 pm and 4-6 pm, Sat 10 am-2 pm. **Real Escuela Andaluza del Arte Ecuestre**, riding school, Av. Duque de Abrantes, tel. 956311100, horse shows Tue and Thu at noon, training Mon, Wed and Fri 11 am-1 pm. **Centro** and **Fundación Andaluza de Flamenco**, Pl. de San Juan 1, flamenco museum and venue for flamenco dance and guitar courses, Mon-Fri 9:30 am-1:30 pm (in winter 10 am-2 pm).

🎻 Flamenco bars: Peña Tio José de Paula, C/ La Merced. **Camino del Rocío**, C/ Velázquez 20.

🍷 Bodega tours (Mon-Fri): **Sandeman**, 12 and 1 pm; **Williams**, 1:30 pm; **Harveys**, 12 pm.

CASTELLAR DE LA FRONTERA

▣ ⊕⊕ Casa Convento La Almoraima, tel. 95669 3002, monastery hotel surrounded by cork-oak forests.

PUERTO DE SANTA MARÍA

i C/ Guadalete 1, tel. 956 542413.

▣ ⊕⊕⊕ Monasterio San Miguel, Larga 27, tel. 966540440, fax 956542604, exclusive hotel in a former monastery.

⊕⊕ Los Cántaros, C/ Curva 6, tel. 956540240, fax 956541121.

🏛 Iglesia Mayor Prioral, daily 10 am-12 pm and 7:30-8:30 pm. **Castillo San Marcos**, Sat 11 am-1 pm.

🍷 Bodega tours: Mon-Fri 9:30 am-1 pm, **Osborne**, tel. 956855211; **Terry**, tel. 956483000.

RONDA (Málaga Province)

i Pl. de España 1, tel. 952871272.

▣ ⊕⊕⊕ Parador de Turismo de Ronda, Pza. de España s/n, tel. 952877500, fax 952878188, tastefully decorated parador. **Reina Victoria**, C/ Jerez 25, tel. 952871240, fax 952871075, traditional hotel, lavishly praised by the poet R. M. Rilke.

⊕⊕ Don Miguel, Villanueva 8, tel. 9528777722, fax 952878377, friendly place, good value for the money.

🏛 Palacio del Marqués La Atalayade Salvatierra, Fri-Wed 11 am-2 pm and 4-7 pm.

SANLÚCAR DE BARRAMEDA

i Calzada de Ejército, Mon-Fri 10 am-2 pm and 5-7 pm, tel. 956366110.

🎫 Visits to **Coto de Doñana National Park through Turafrica, C/ San Juan, tel. 956362540.

TARIFA

▣ ⊕⊕ Hurricane, Ctra. de Cádiz, km 77, tel. 956684919, exclusive sports hotel right on the beach.

VEJER

▣ ⊕⊕ Convento San Francisco, Plazuela, tel. 956451001, fax 956451004, charming monastery hotel.

ZAHARA DE LA SIERRA / GRAZALEMA

▣ ⊕⊕ Marqués de Zahara, C/ San Juan 3, tel. 956123061. **Villa Turística**, Grazalema, El Olivar, tel. 956132162, fax 956132213.

Andalusia

**SEVILLA

Metropolis of the South

As the saying goes: *Quién no ha visto Sevilla, no ha visto maravilla* ("He who has not seen Sevilla has seen no wonders at all"). **Sevilla** ㉕ (pop. 700,000), situated 10 meters above sea level on the sedate Guadalquivir River and capital of Andalusia, was at one time an important commercial harbor. In summer, there is no hotter place in all of Spain.

Sevilla's emblem is the Giralda, originally the minaret on the Almohad mosque, and today the bell tower on the largest Gothic cathedral in the world. East and West mix in a vast melting pot called the Alcázar, where Islamic artists once carried out commissions for Christian patrons. Mysterious squares and tiny streets lined with white houses harboring small green oases called *patios* (courtyards) impregnate the atmosphere of the Old Town. Sevillans love to mingle in their plazas, which, come evening, turn into large open-air cafés. The day's cares are forgotten, the waiter brings glasses of sherry to the table, and then comes the difficult decision – which of the many delicious tapas to order, all so temptingly arrayed at the bar.

Sevillans are lively, life-loving people, geniuses at turning any religious or secular occasion into a *fiesta*, a celebration. The most important is the **Feria de Abril*. Originally a cattle market, 1,000 *casetas*, elaborately decorated tents, are raised annually for the sole purpose of singing and dancing with utter abandon until the early morning hours. Serious participants dress in traditional costume: Carmen and Don Juan are born again.

The second most important fiesta is **Semana Santa* (Holy Week): a fusion of the religious and the secular, a celebra-

tion unlike anything else on earth revolving around processions organized by the *cofradías* (confraternities). Musicians accompany the processions, some beating out an austere drum-roll, others carrying *pasos,* floats on which scenes from the Passion are depicted. As many as 50 float-bearers called *costaleros* are needed to carry the extremely heavy *pasos,* and when they make the Christ or Virgin Mary figures "dance," the spectators applaud. Penitents wander barefoot over carpets of flowers, wearing or bearing (as the case may be) chains, crosses, candles and hair shirts. Silent processions shuffle slowly through the narrow streets, their progress punctuated only by the sound of flamenco songs (*saetas*) performed by believers to the acclaim of the crowd. When the processions are over, Sevillans throng to restaurants and bars, which remain open all night.

History

Founded by the Phoenicians and later captured by Julius Caesar, Sevilla was a district capital in the Roman province of Baetica. During this period the city and river were named Hispalis and Betis respectively. Under the Visigoths, the official conversion of Spain from Arianism to Catholicism began here. The heir to the throne, San Hermenegildo, as well as bishops San Isidoro and San Leandro, spread the Gospel in the 6th century. The Islamic rulers changed both the face of the city and its name (to Isbiliat) and gave the river the name it bears today. Beginning in the 11th century Sevilla was the seat of the Emirs of the Almohad Dynasty, and in 1248 Ferdinand III of Castile conquered the city, thereby bringing Islamic domination to an end.

In the 16th century Sevilla became Spain's wealthiest city and transhipment center for goods coming from the colonies, including the coveted commodities silver and gold. The bustling port at-

Left: Even the youngest wear flowers in their hair and festive costumes for the Feria de Abril.

Andalusia

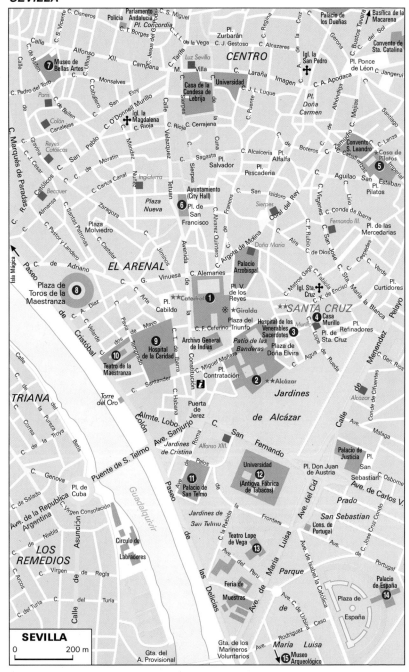

tracted not only export and import merchants, but also charlatans, vagabonds and rogues. Cultural activities increased apace, and the ambitious project of building the world's largest Gothic cathedral was undertaken. The gifted sculptors Martínez Montañes and Nuño Delgado, the master woodcarver Rodrigo Alemán and the incomparable painters Murillo, Zurbarán, Valdés Leal and Velázquez rose to prominence through the work they did here. In literature, the Sevilla School flourished under the patronage of the House of Gelves, descendants of Columbus. Some of the greatest poets of the Renaissance, such as De Herrera, Aldana and De la Torre were active in the city. Four centuries later, the Generation of '27 revived this tradition.

The first flush of colonial fever subsided under Bourbon rule. Charles III, desirous that future generations have access to the historical record, ordered the establishment of the Archivo General de Indias on the second floor of the old Merchants' Exchange, a 16th-century building by Juan de Herrera, with the result that many colonial documents still await discovery by students of the period. After its port silted up, Sevilla lost its trading monopoly with America to Cádiz in 1717, and it was not until the advent of industrialization that the city recovered from this severe blow to its economic fortunes. In 1929, the Ibero-American Exposition was held in the city, and by a strange twist of numerological fate, Sevilla was also the site of Expo '92. But these events did not provide sufficient impetus to bring about the hoped-for economic revival in southern Spain.

Sevilla's Old Town

The ground plan of Sevilla's **★★Cathedral ❶**, built on the site of the

Above: The Torre de Oro is one of Sevilla's most famous landmarks.

former Almohad mosque, measures 116 x 76 meters, making it (according to the *Guinness Book of Records)* the world's third-largest church. In 1506, the Cathedral was consecrated after over 100 years of construction. It has nine portals, five naves reaching 36 meters in height, 45 side chapels and the largest altarpiece in Christendom. The **Retablo**, is based on a design dating from 1482 by the Flemish sculptor Pieter Dancart. In the center of the Cathedral, encircled by representations of the salvation history, stands the majestic *Virgen de la Sede*, the patron saint of the Cathedral. Behind the Capilla Mayor in the Plateresque **Capilla Real** is the tomb of Saint Ferdinand, Ferdinand III of Castile, who recaptured Sevilla from the Moors in 1248. He is flanked by his wife, Beatrice of Swabia and his son Alfonso the Wise. The 13th-century statue of the patron saint of Sevilla, the *Virgen de los Reyes*, is also venerated in this chapel.

In front of the **Puerta de San Cristobal** stands the imposing tomb built

in 1902 in honor of the great explorer Cristóbal Colón (Christopher Columbus). Whether or not the mariner's bones actually repose here cannot be said with absolute certainty, for after his death in 1506 his mortal remains went (with Spain's approval) on a 400-year-long post-mortem odyssey that took them to Valladolid, Sevilla, Santo Domingo, Havana and finally back to Sevilla.

The **sacristy** houses a superb silver monstrance by Juan de Arfe, as well as fine paintings by Murillo, Valdés Leal and Zurbarán. Also worth seeing is the unusual elliptical **chapter house** dating from the 16th century, with a dome adorned with Baroque frescoes.

The **Puerta de Perdón** (Portal of Forgiveness) leads to the **Patio de los Naranjos** (Orange-Tree Courtyard), like the Giralda a survivor of the mosque that

Above: The richly-gilded Retablo in the Cathedral of Sevilla. Right: The Giralda, originally the minaret of the old mosque, as depicted in a 16th-century painting.

once stood here, which was used for ritual ablutions by the Muslims. On the east side of the courtyard is the **Biblioteca Colombina**, a bequest by Columbus' son Hernando Colón.

From the **★★Giralda**, originally the minaret of the mosque and now the bell tower of the Cathedral, there is a fantastic panorama over the entire city. The Moorish-style structure, which was built in the 12th century during the Almohad Dynasty, resembles the diamond-shaped *sebka* minarets of Rabat and Marrakesh, although the quadrilateral brick tower dating from the Renaissance considerably altered its appearance. Other additions from this period include the balconies, a belfry and a weather vane representing *giraldillo* (faith), from which the tower derives its name. The Giralda reaches a height of 100 meters, and can comfortably be ascended to 70 meters by means of a ramp which Ferdinand III triumphantly mounted on horseback after taking Sevilla in 1248. The more than 140 diminutive columns

adorning the exterior of the tower originally came from the Palace of Medina Azahara at Córdoba.

South of the Cathedral stands the **Archivo General de Indias**, which contains extensive documentation on the conquest of the New World.

It's almost impossible not to notice the lion's gate facing the Archivo through which visitors enter the ★★**Alcázar** ❷, the former palace of the Almohads. Following the Reconquest, it became the royal seat of the kings of Castile, and was renovated in the 14th century under King Pedro I. For this undertaking, Pedro employed Granadan craftsmen from the court of his ally, the Nasrid ruler Mohammed V, with the result that in certain respects the Alcázar resembles the Alhambra. In the 16th century the palace was expanded under Charles V, and in the 19th century it underwent a thorough restoration.

To the right of the palace gate is the **Casa de la Contratación**, which Isabella I established in 1503 in order to direct the

administration and trade of Spain's overseas colonies. Here, the Virgen de los Navegantes, patron saint of mariners, protectively drapes her coat over Columbus and his caravels from the vantage point of a winged altar.

The actual palace complex is built around two interior courtyards: the impressive Patio de las Doncellas was the scene of public life, while in the smaller and more intimate Patio de las Muñecas private life unfolded. The pearl of the palace is without doubt the Sala de los Embajadores, the Ambassadors' Hall. An almost surrealistically star-studded dome of larch wood spans this quadrilateral space whose walls are delightfully decorated with azulejo tiles and filigree stucco-work arabesques in warm colors. The room was also the sumptuous scene of the wedding of Charles V and Isabella of Portugal.

The sections of the palace built under Charles I are most notable for the 12 superb and very large tapestries that evoke the emperor's Tunisian campaign.

The **Jardines de Alcázar**, an otherworldly oasis of peace in the midst of a bustling urban environment, are perhaps the most famous gardens in the world – and with good reason. Here, the genius of Moorish horticulture gives the Renaissance, and modernity, a run for its money. The air is redolent with orange blossoms; vibrant bougainvillea and magnolia blossoms gladden the eye, while the gentle murmer of perfectly calibrated fountains soothes the soul.

The atmospheric former Jewish quarter, **★★Barrio de Santa Cruz**, lies just behind the battlement-crowned Moorish walls. Already in 1391 angry Christian mobs, incited by the harangues of fanatic preachers, went on a rampage through the Jewish merchants' and craftsmen's quarter, which at that time extended far beyond the present-day Barrio.

Above: The Ambassadors' Hall in the Alcázar – a jewel of Moorish decorative art. Right: A procession of penitents during Semana Santa.

This pogrom sealed the fate of Sevilla's Jewish community. The survivors were driven out, and the synagogues torn down or converted into churches. Extensive restoration work carried out in the 20th century saved the quarter from becoming irreversibly dilapidated and transformed it into the architectural jewel that it is today. Within the maze of narrow streets and nostalgic squares visitors encounter cozy restaurants and traditonal bars, as well as small pensions and shops with fascinating merchandise ranging from kitsch to fine arts and crafts.

The most appealing approach to the Santa Cruz district lies east of the **Patio de las Banderas**, which is where visitors emerge from the Alcázar. From there a small covered street leads into the former Jewish quarter. Some of the loveliest Sevillan patios are located on **Callejón de Agua** (Water Alley), where the **Acueducta** that once brought this district water can still be seen.

In the 16th century, **Plaza de Doña Elvira**, with its handsomely tiled benches,

was used as an open-air theater where the audience could follow the action from their balconies. The Baroque **Hospital de los Venerables Sacerdotes** ❸ on Plaza de Los Venerables once served as an old age and nursing home for priests past their prime and is now used for art exhibitions. **Plaza de Santa Cruz**, where a beautifully-crafted wrought iron cross now stands, was formerly the site of the church in which the painter Murillo was buried. **Casa Murillo** ❹, the artist's former residence, is only a matter of steps away from the **Convento de las Decalzas**, a Carmelite convent that was founded in the 16th century by the originator of the Carmelite Reformation, Saint Teresa of Avila. Traditionally attributed to her is the statement that anyone who succeeds in living without sin in a city that tempts the senses as sorely as Sevilla does deserves the highest respect.

Walking north of Barrio Santa Cruz takes you to the ★**Casa de Pilatos** ❺, the most spectacular nobleman's palace in Sevilla, commissioned in the early 16th century by the royal governor Don Pedro Enríquez and his son Don Fadrique. With its handsome arcaded courtyard, the structure brilliantly combines Renaissance, Flamboyant Gothic and Mudéjar architectural elements. The walls of the entire palace are tiled with marvelous 16th-century azulejos which, like the gardens, bring the Alcázar vividly to mind. In the courtyard, groups of Greek and Roman statues are arrayed around an elegant fountain, and the walls are adorned with the busts of 24 Roman emperors. Today the palace is owned by the Dukes of Medinaceli. Because of this, the apartments on the upper floor can only be visited in the family's absence.

The center of Sevilla is divided into two areas – Plaza Nueva and **Plaza San Francisco**, the latter of which boasts an impressive **Ayuntamiento** ❻ (City Hall), before which the annual Semana Santa processions pass in review under the watchful and bemused eyes of the assembled pillars of the community. From here, the town's main pedestrian shopping street, **Calle Sierpes**, begins. In summer it is graced with awnings to keep the scorching Andalusian sun at bay.

At the western edge of the city center, near the river and the former Córdoba railroad station, is the **Museo de Bellas Artes ❼**, which contains the second largest collection of paintings in Spain (after the Prado). The museum building began life as a Baroque monastery and is a work of art in its own right. The museum's holdings encompass works by Spanish and Italian painters from the 15th to 18th centuries, and especially such Andalusian artists of the Baroque period as Murillo, Valdés Leal and Zurbarán.

At the northern tip of the Old Town, visitors who want to get real for a while can hang out in the working class **Barrio de la Macarena**, where the old city wall is astoundingly well preserved. The **Basílica de la Macarena** houses the "diva" of Sevillan Madonnas, the Virgen de la Macarena, who has her "big moment" during Holy Week. In a museum adjoining the Basilica the Madonna's fine raiments and sumptuous jewels can be admired.

Neighboring **San Lorenzo** is another working-class stronghold. It is concentrated around the church of the same name, which contains a much admired statue of Christ, *El Gran Poder.* In a more secular vein, on Sundays the **Alameda de Hercules** is the site of a flea market at which, it is said, a mind-boggling range of stolen goods changes hands.

Along the Guadalquivir River

A footpath leads from the Cathedral to the river by way of that most delightful of districts, **El Arenal**.

A great pleasure it is indeed to meander along the elegant riverbank promenade to the **Plaza de Toros de la Maestranza ❽**

Right: The entire city of Sevilla dresses in festive costumes to celebrate the Feria de Abril.

(bullring), which is steeped in tradition and counts as one of the most beautiful in all of Spain. The exhibits in the attached museum revolve around the death-defying sport of bullfighting.

The **Hospital de la Caridad ❾** was erected in the 17th century with the aid of generous bequests from Don Miguel de Mañara, a member of the Order of the Good Samaritans. Still carrying out its original mission today, the hospital, run as in the past by the brothers of the order, provides shelter and medical care to senior citizens of limited means. Murillo and Valdés Leal, two of the greatest artists of the time, were enlisted to decorate the church. Murillo created a compelling cycle of paintings depicting the friars and their merciful works, while the very scent of decomposing flesh makes its presence palpably felt in Valdés' contribution, so persuasively has he incarnated the theme of *memento mori* ("remember that you must die").

Once past the modern concert and opera house **Teatro de la Maestranza ❿**, which was built for Expo '92, follow your nose to the Guadalquivir River, where a twelve-faceted Almohad watchtower built in 1220 known as the **Torre del Oro** rises grandly towards heaven. The appellation "golden tower" harks back to the time when the tower's dome was covered with golden tiles. Inside is a **Museo Marítimo** of modest proportions that reflects back on Sevilla's 16th-century salad days when it was a major commercial and transhipment center.

Ages ago the haunt of mariners, potters and gypsies, the **Triana** quarter (on the right bank of the river) has remained true to its traditions and still extends a warm embrace to the "common man" (and woman). Hand-made pottery has long been produced in this district, and **Plaza Callao** contains innumerable workshops steeped in a venerable tradition of fine crafts. There are so many seafood restaurants on **Calle del Betis** that it's difficult

Andalusia

to choose one, especially because they all offer romantic panoramas of nocturnally illuminated Sevilla from their outdoor terraces.

A short distance to the north lies the island of Cartuja, which derives its name from the former 14th-century Carthusian monastery **La Cartuja de Santa María de las Cuevas**. It was here that Columbus brooded over his itinerary and that, with the advent of secularization, an Englishman named Pickman opened a ceramics factory in 1836 which produced pots until 1982. The monastery was extensively remodeled and opened to the public for Expo '92, and the island itself was a major exhibition area during the event and much in the media limelight. Before Expo opened, controversy was stirred up over its "500th Anniversary of the Discovery of America" theme. The high hopes pinned on Expo for the island's economic resurrection unfortunately came to little. There had been talk of converting it into a technology park, but in the end it became an amusement center

called **Isla Mágica** instead. However, the remains of the Expo infrastructure have benefited Sevilla: seven new bridges now span the Guadalquivir, the high-speed AVE trains link Sevilla and Madrid, and the airport was also expanded.

South of the Old Town

Puerta de Jerez, named after a city gate destroyed long ago, is today one of the busiest traffic junctions in Sevilla as well as the starting point for a walking tour south of the Old Town.

Located on **Avenida de Roma** facing the Jardines de Santa Cristina, the Baroque **Palacio de San Telmo** ⑪ was, in times past, a training academy for aspiring mariners. It later served as residence for the Dukes of Montpensier. The palace was designed in 1734 by Leonardo de Figueroa. The architect apparently took particular care with the three-level portal: San Telmo, the patron saint of mariners, soberly surveys the Guadalquivir from an open arcade.

Having passed by Sevilla's most exclusive hotel, the **Alfonso XIII**, which was built in 1929 at the time of the Ibero-American Exposition, you come upon the **University ⑫**, which in the 18th century was a municipal tobacco processing factory. Built around innumerable courtyards, this huge palatial complex is the second largest secular construction in Spain – after the El Escorial monastery near Madrid. Some of the sentry houses where the workers were checked as they left the factory have been preserved. Legend has it that among the 10,000 *cigarreras* laboring here was the fiery-eyed Carmen, who achieved immortality by inspiring the author Prosper Mérimée's gripping novella and later Georges Bizet's opera.

Facing the **Teatro Lope de Vega ⑬** are the "green lungs" of Sevilla, the **Parque de María Luisa**, a priceless oasis on a

Above: The wonderful mosaics of Plaza de España recount the history of the Spanish provinces.

scorching summer day. Until 1893, this veritable Garden of Eden was part of the palace of San Telmo. Sevillans owe a debt of gratitude to María Luisa, sister of Isabella II and mistress of the Palacio de San Telmo, for it was she who decided that all residents of Sevilla should be allowed into the park. In 1929, the French landscape architect Le Forestier reconfigured the entire area for the Ibero-American Exposition.

On weekends, the **Plaza de España** provides Sevillan wedding couples with just the right imposing backdrop against which to snap the first photos for their family albums. The hemispheric **Palacio de España ⑭**, with its striking corner towers that are replicas of the Giralda's, was the main attraction at the 1929 Exposition. Painted tiles adorning the base of the structure instruct and delight visitors with depictions of scenes from the history of Spain's provinces.

Plaza de América at the south end of the park is the location of the **Museo de Artes y Costumbres Populares** and the

Museo Arqueológico ⑮. The former documents how the common people used to dress, the tools they once used and the furniture they furnished their homes with. The latter institution's holdings include the fruits of excavations in the nearby Roman ruins of Itálica, as well as the gold treasure of Carambolo, which dates back to the 7th and 8th centuries B.C.

As evening draws nigh, floodlights take over where the sun left off, drenching the park's squares, the Cathedral, the Alcázar and the Torre del Oro in warm light. From the Giralda, visitors can take a romatic horse-drawn carriage ride through the veritable fairyland of nocturnal Sevilla.

The Ruins of Itálica

The *Colonia Aelia Augusta Itálica ㉖, the most ancient Roman settlement excavated in Spain to date, is located only nine kilometers from Sevilla near the town of Santiponce. The settlement was founded in 206 B.C. by the Roman general Publius Cornelius Scipio for the benefit of veterans of the Second Punic War. Before long, the ex-warriors put down roots and began marrying the local women. Mercantile success soon followed, and Itálica developed into a thriving commercial center that later supplied Rome with the emperors Trajan (b. A.D. 53) and Hadrian (b. A.D. 76). The fall of the Roman Empire precipitated a decline in the city's fortunes. When the Moors came to power, Itálica was abandoned, after which it became a quarry for neighboring towns. The first major archaeological excavations were carried out in the early 20th century.

On either side of the main axis of the former residential area, which was built under Hadrian, foundations of sizeable villas can be clearly discerned. Of particular interest are the striking, virtually intact mosaics, although in recent years many have been covered or removed in order to forestall damage from the environment. There are plans to incorporate them in the near future into the Itálica wing of Sevilla's Archaeological Museum. An elliptical stone colossus lying at the foot of the hill on which the Roman city was located, the 160 x 137-meter **Anfiteatro** (amphitheater) could seat 25,000 spectators in its heyday. Only the Colosseum in Rome and the arena in Capua are larger.

HUELVA PROVINCE

From an economic standpoint, this westernmost province of Andalusia is one step ahead of the crowd. On huge fields, early vegetables and strawberries destined for all of Europe ripen in plastic tunnels. The provincial city (as opposed to the province) of Huelva is a center of petrochemical activity. The province's most notable attraction is the Coto de Doñana National Park.

The City of Huelva –
The Industrial Heart of Andalusia

Though the provincial capital of **Huelva** ㉗ (population 130,000) dates back to Roman times, no traces of the city's ancient roots remain: tremors from the Lisbon earthquake of 1755 spared only the 16th-century churches of **San Pedro** and **La Concepción**. Copper and tin from the mines at Ríotinto brought prosperity to the city long ago, and minerals are still processed here. But the petrochemical and paper industries, the main sources of revenue these days, are slowly turning the bay into a cesspool.

From the Marismas to Portugal

In summer the sandy beaches west of the city are used primarily by local residents. On the westward-lying spit of land at the broad mouth of the Odiel and Tinto rivers is **Punta Umbría**. From here to the

Andalusia

Portuguese border visitors can count on finding an uninterrupted series of broad beaches, small resorts, sand dunes and pine forests.

Above Punta Umbría are the Odiel marshlands, the *marismas*, which resemble those of the Coto de Doñana. The topography of the terrain, which is regularly flooded by the restless tides, undergoes constant change, thereby creating a variegated habitat for the endemic flora and fauna.

The ocean currents shifting river sediment build up long barrier islands parallel to the coast, creating such Edenic venues for swimmers as the more than ten-kilometer-long island at the mouth of the Piedras River. It can be reached from **El Rompido**, where extensive fish and mussel hatcheries have been established in the river's long tidal zone.

Isla Cristina and **Isla Canela** are other well-frequented seaside resorts with superb beaches and first-rate seafood restaurants. Located at the mouth of the Guadiana River, which forms the border with Portugal, **Ayamonte 28** is an important fishing port and the last town in Spain. The terraced white houses culminate in a parador at the top of the hill. It is in an old monastery with a view of the sea and the countless coves and sandbanks in the estuary. A recently-built bridge allows travelers to cross over the Guadiana to Portugal.

The Columbian Route

As you leave Huelva heading west, you soon come upon the monumental **Columbus Memorial** (1929) by the American sculptress Gertrude Whitney, a gift from the United States to Huelva, and the beginning of the so-called **Columbian Route**. The name is a reminder that the

Right. A pair of breeding whiskered terns (Chlidonias hybrida) at the Coto de Doñana National Park.

great navigator set out on his voyages of discovery from this region at the end of the 15th century.

In the years before Columbus obtained financial support from Ferdinand and Isabella, the Franciscan monastery of **La Rábida**, whose origins date back to the 14th century, served as his refuge from the outside world. It contains paintings and other memorabilia from the time Columbus spent among the monks. He also named one of his caravels after Santa María de la Rábida, the patron saint of the monastery.

Avenida América takes you from the Franciscan monastery to the town of **Palos de la Frontera 29**. The harbor (long ago silted up) of the tiny village is the place from which Columbus and the Palos-born Pinzón brothers set out for the New World in their three caravels on August 3, 1492. Before weighing anchor, they prayed for success and God's protection in the 15th-century church of **San Jorge**. Since 1992, 500 years after the discovery of the New World, this great event has been commemorated by models of the caravels Columbus sailed in, the **Muelle de las Carabelas**, and an adjacent museum brings the voyage vividly to life with a multivision presentation.

The first Mass Columbus attended upon returning from America was celebrated at the **Convento de Santa Clara** (14th century) in **Moguer 30**, a few kilometers inland. The church is decorated with Mudéjar elements, the loveliest of which is a small statue of Jesus, *La Roldana,* by the Baroque artist Luisa Roldán. Her little-known sculptures, on display in area churches, are well worth seeking out.

Nobel prize laureate Juan Ramón Jiménez (1881-1958) immortalized his home town of Moguer with the philosophical dialogues *Platero y Yo*. Moguer, prettily ornamented with the typical white houses of the region, is fond of reminding visitors about its illustrious na-

Andalusia

tive son, and the poet's former home is now a museum.

★★Coto de Doñana and Environs

Pine forests line the kilometers-long sand beaches between Huelva and the Coto de Doñana National Park, a stretch of coast with virtually no real towns. **Matalascañas ③**, built for tourists and the major vacation resort on this stretch of coast, bursts at the seams in summer and shrinks to ghostly proportions in the off-season. Environmentalists have successfully blocked further development of the "town," whose tourist trade constitutes a threat to the ecological balance of the nearby national park.

In 1969, **★★Coto de Doñana National Park** was created out of the ecologically endangered 50,000-hectare Guadalquivir estuary. Owing to the abundance of its animal population, royal personages favored the area for hunting from the late 16th century on. Before the area became a park, local farmers had drained parts of

its marshlands and had converted the eastern section into rice fields. The drainage had put flora and fauna at risk, and encroachment on the area by tourist facilities had exacerbated the problem. This marshland, containing countless river-nourishing watercourses, is one of the most important waterfowl reserves in Europe, owing to the fact that it lies at the border of two continents and therefore serves as a migration rest stop for approximately 250 species.

Beyond the *marismas* (marshlands) lie two other ecosystems girdled by sand dunes and Mediterranean coppice in which lynx, roe deer, red deer and wild boar live.

Visitors to the park are subject to strict regulations. Short hikes are permitted near the information centers located along the road from Almonte to the coast, where well-marked paths and observation platforms tucked away amongst the marshes promote quality bird-watching. Visitors wishing to learn more about the park's vegetation can opt for a half-day tour in an off-road vehicle, which can be booked at the **El Acebuche** information center.

Every Whitsun, hundreds of thousands of pilgrims converge on the village of **El Rocio** ❷ to pay homage to the *Paloma Blanca,* the "White Dove," as the Madonna of Rocío is called. The miracle-working Madonna, who constitutes the only tourist attraction in this white-washed village, has been an object of veneration since the l3th century. Over the years, the pilgrimage has evolved into a high-spirited festival. Each year, 78 different confraternities dress in traditional garb and travel here in ox-drawn carts in order to participate in the event.

After the intensely spiritual three days have ended and the brotherhoods have departed from their houses, a Wild West atmosphere prevails in the village for a time.

Sierra de Aracena

In a remote comer of northwestern Andalusia, in the foothills of the Sierra Morena mountains, rise the **Sierra de Aracena**, a series of hills interspersed with small villages. Some are mining towns, while others are primarily clusters of weekend homes belonging to residents of Huelva and Sevilla. The vegetation consists primarily of holm and cork oak, mimosa and chestnut, and large areas covered with maquis and rockroses. In sparsely populated areas of the region, such animals as vultures, imperial eagles, and even the extremely rare Iberian lynx seek refuge.

Copper is mined at **Zalamea la Real** ❸. The red terraces of open cast mining color the Tinto (ink) River, which flows into the Atlantic at Huelva.

The largest **Museo Minero** (mining museum) in Europe recently opened its

doors in **Ríotinto** ❹. To ensure authenticity, visitors are transported through the exhibit in mining trucks.

The most important town in the Sierra is **Aracena** ❺; above it rises an Arab fortress, as well as a Gothic church with a Mudéjar tower. Deep within the mountain crowned by the fortress are the **Grutas de las Maravillas** – extensive caverns with subterranean lakes and dripstone formations that are the stuff of dreams.

The town of **Jabugo** ❻ has bestowed its name upon Spain's tastiest mountain hams, made here from half-wild black pigs fattened for the kill on acorns, which is all the animals ever eat.

In addition to prehistoric finds and well-preserved city walls, **Acroche** ❼ has the curious **Museo de los Rosarios** (Rosary Museum). This is also the northern gateway to the expanses of the Meseta and Extremadura.

Carmona – Treasure Chamber of the Guadalquivir Plain

Carmona ❽ lies on a 250-meter-high ridge rising out of the fields of sunflowers and cereal grains that are cultivated on the Guadalquivir River plain below. Early in its history, Carmona was a flourishing center of trade owing to its strategic location, reaching its peak under the Romans, who granted the city the right to mint coins and erected fortifications, some of which have successfully withstood the ravages of time.

Carmona's main street, which was once part of the Roman Via Augusta, leads through the town's massive Moorish city gate, the **Puerta de Sevilla**, straight to the circular **Plaza de San Fernando**. Of the square's numerous venerable buildings, the **Town Hall** is most noteworthy for the Roman mosaic of a Medusa's head found inside the building. A few steps away is the 15th-century church of **Santa María la Mayor**, which was built on the founda-

Right: Andalusians are especially proud of their horses.

tions of the principal mosque, of which the orange-tree courtyard has survived. A calendar from the 6th century is inscribed on one of the columns in the church courtyard, itself a vestige of an earlier Visigoth structure.

The **Parador**, once the preferred residence of King Pedro I, sits high up on the ridge. Its terrace affords a superb vista of the surrounding countryside.

The **Necrópolis Romana**, used by the Romans as a burial site from the 2nd to 4th centuries A.D., sits imposingly before the old city gates. Some 250 of the over 1,000 graves have been excavated to date. Of the family mausoleums outfitted with niches for urns and household gods, the **Tumba de Servilia** is larger and more lavishly "furnished" than any excavated so far. Worth having a look at as well is the **Tumba del Elefante**, which is adorned with the statue of a small elephant, a symbol of longevity. The museum adjoining the excavations provides some interesting information on Roman burial rites.

Ecija –
City of Towers

Amidst the fertile fields of the Guadalquivir River valley lies the handsome town of **Ecija** ㊴. The most traumatic event in its long history was without doubt the Lisbon earthquake of 1755, which reduced the city to rubble and ashes. Ecija owes its overwhelmingly Baroque character to its having been completely rebuilt in the latter half of the 18th century, since which time storks have developed a penchant for nesting in the town's Baroque church towers – whereby decision-making can prove somewhat difficult for the storks, as there are 12 towers for them to choose from.

The former palaces of large landowners lend the town a stately, dignified air. The **Palacio de Peñaflor**, which reputedly has the longest balcony in Spain, is now home to a cultural center. The **Palacio de los Marqueses de Benamejí** features stately courtyards containing a collection of coaches.

The heart of Ecija is the **Plaza de España**, whose Town Hall houses an admirable Roman mosaic dating from 2 B.C. In the square itself there is always a ready supply of men discussing the day's events in rapid Spanish punctuated by highly expressive body language.

CÓRDOBA
Seat of Power of the Caliphs of Al-Andaluz

Córdoba 40 was once the jewel in the crown of the Caliphate of Al-Andaluz, a metropolis on the banks of the Guadalquivir River where culture, the sciences and trade flourished; a place to which pilgrims journeyed from throughout the Islamic world; a city that was bursting at the seams with a population, it has been said, of almost one million, gargantuan for the period, and over three times today's comparatively meager

Above: The dome of the Mezquita – a display of consummate architectural and artistic skill.

300,000. But in the year 1031, the Caliphate self-destructed as a result of internal power struggles. The Medina Azahara, the palace complex at the city gates, was razed to the ground by Berber troops, and Córdoba was henceforth overshadowed by Sevilla. After the city was conquered by Ferdinand III in 1236, it was used by the Christians as a staging point for further conquests.

Córdoba has since been conquered again – by tourists, most of whom come to gaze in rapture at the **Mezquita 1**, the sublime Moorish gift to posterity that was once the principal mosque of Córdoba and is today the Cathedral. The Mezquita counts as one of the supreme achievements of Islamic architecture, though the intensity of the overall effect has been somewhat diminished by Christian additions, which caused irreparable harm to the delightful illusion of seemingly endless forests of marble, jasper and porphyry.

Charles V, who ordered the Cathedral built in 1523 despite fierce opposition

CÓRDOBA

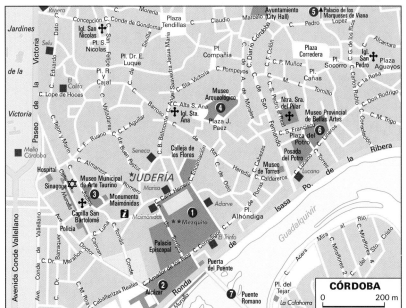

Andalusia

among the populace, is reported to have said during a later visit to Córdoba: "What has been built here could have been built anywhere, but what has been destroyed could not possibly be re-created."

The 23,000-square-meter vastness of the Mezquita made it the third-largest mosque in the world at the time of its completion. The double-tiered, scalloped arches patterned with alternating striations of stone and brick divide the interior into no fewer than 19 aisles, each of which is 175 meters long.

The pillars especially reflect the various building phases: In the oldest section of the Cathedral, built in 785 under Emir Abd ar-Rahman I, Visigothic and Roman church capitals were used, and for the extension to the present-day Cathedral area, pillars from ancient Roman buildings were incorporated. Blue and pink marble quarried from the surrounding countryside was polished and worked for the third extension, which contains only Corinthian capitals. The *mihrab*, a prayer

niche facing Mecca, is situated along the aisle in the *kibla* wall, spanned by a remarkable dome that is covered with myriad tiny, glittering mosaic tiles. This is without doubt the most exquisite part of the Mezquita.

The final expansion of the mosque, enlarging it by eight ailes – from 11 to its present 19 – was carried out under Commander Almansor, who dispensed with salaried craftsmen and had slaves brought in to do the work instead. Consequently, the architecture in this part of the mosque is not as accomplished as in the rest of the structure.

The Cathedral, which towers over the austere roofs of the mosque, was designed by master builder Hernán Ruíz in the 16th century. Most noteworthy inside are the magnificent mahogany choir stalls by the sculptor Pedro Duque de Cornejo. Next to the choir are the superb chapels of Real and Villaviciosa. The former vestibule of the mosque, the Orange-Tree Courtyard, still contains the building's original minaret.

Situated on lovely riverside grounds behind the mosque, the **Alcázar ❷**, with its majestic towers, was home to the Catholic Monarchs during the conquest of Granada. They also received their first visit from Columbus here in 1486. Sessions of the courts of the Spanish Inquisition were also held within these fortifications.

The well-preserved Arab city wall behind the Alcázar leads to Puerta de Almodóvar, the entrance to the former Jewish quarter, the **★Judería**, which extends as far as the mosque and was one of the largest Jewish communities in Spain. Its narrow winding streets with simple whitewashed houses from which flowers picturesquely spill over their window boxes is a gladdening sight, particularly on Calleja de las Flores (Flower Lane), a picture postcard come to life.

Only one synagogue, a Mudéjar-style building from the 14th century, has been preserved. Nearby is the **monument** to the famed philospher and scholar Rabbi Moses Ben Maimon (1135-1204), known as **Maimonides**, who was a native of Córdoba, as was his contemporary, the Arab philosopher Averroes (1126-1198). But even in Roman times, Córdoba gave the world such learned men as the two Senecas and the poet Lucanus. Diagonally opposite the Maimonides monument is the **Museo Municipal de Arte Taurino ❸**, which pays tribute to such legendary Córdoban toreros as Manolete and Lagartijo.

The sections of Córdoba bordering the mosque and Judería, with their narrow, twisting streets, are palpably Arabic in character. In order to reach its present-day proportions, Córdoba was forced to expand beyond these older districts. In the Old Town, visitors will encounter numerous churches whose bell towers

Right. Brightly-colored flowers can be seen everywhere in Córdoba, especially on Calleja de las Flores.

clearly began life as minarets. The streets and lanes open onto one lovely square after another. Among them are **Plaza del Potro**, which has a fountain adorned with a stone horse and an inn named after the square where Don Quixote is said to have spent the night, and **Plaza de la Corredera**, which evokes the great town squares of Castile.

A host of monasteries and palaces testifies to Córdoba's illustrious past. The **Museo Arqueológico ❹**, with its exhibitions of artifacts from the Roman, Visigothic and Arabic epochs, is today housed inside the **Palacio Paéz de Quijano**.

Northeast of Plaza de la Corredera in the **Palacio de los Marqueses de Viana ❺**, with its 13 festively floral courtyards, visitors can get a feel for the lifestyle of the Andalusian nobility of yesteryear. The **Museo Provincial de Bellas Artes ❻** in the old **Hospital de la Caridad** has a few works by such renowned artists as Zurbarán, Rivera and Murillo.

The **Puente Romana ❼** (Roman Bridge), built during the reign of Emperor Augustus, still spans the Guadalquivir River. At one end of the bridge, the **La Calahorra** watchtower offers visitors a lively multimedia survey of Córdoba's action-packed history.

★★Medina Azahara – Palace City of the Caliphs

Just outside the old city gates of Córdoba lie the vestiges of **★★Medina Azahara ❹**, the once magnificent palace of the Omayyad Dynasty. Over the course of the past few decades, archaeologists have painstakingly reconstructed sections of the complex from its original components, so that visitors now get a reasonably good feel for the size and splendor of the original.

The palace was built at the behest of Abd ar-Rahman III during the golden age of the Caliphate of Córdoba, but it was

only after 25 years of work that the structure was finally completed in the year 960 during the reign of his son and successor Al Hakem II.

The melodious-sounding name Medina Azahara (City of Flowers) was bestowed upon the palace by Abd ar-Rahman III in honor of his favorite wife, Azahara. According to present-day estimates, around 20,000 people lived and worked within the complex, whose main purpose was to accommodate the royal household.

The palace city was constructed on three levels. The caliph used the upper level as receiving rooms and for his private apartments, while his army inhabited the buildings in the lower levels. **Dar al Yund**, an assembly hall notable for its pristine symmetry, has been well preserved. Ramps lead to a vast parade ground with an amazing portal, which was originally made from 15 horseshoe arches.

The only dissonant architectural note in the complex is the mosque: the founda-

tions are all that have survived of this once ornately decorated five-aisle colonnaded structure. In contrast, the ★**Dar al Mulk** (Ambassadors' Hall), whose magnificent façade was reflected in a huge fountain spread out before it, has been painstakingly reconstructed. Its interior walls are covered with filigree stuccowork, and elegant marble columns linked by horseshoe arches line the three-aisle interior structure. The caliphs entertained many emissaries from abroad in this magnificent hall, which his guests praised highly for its exceptional lavishness in the reports they sent home.

The days of this fairy-tale palace city were numbered, however. In the year 1010, Berber troops descended upon the complex and destroyed almost all of it, a blow which precipitated the demise of the caliphate. Medina Azahara was subsequently used for generation upon generation as a source of building materials, a practice that was only stopped in 1923 when the palace city was declared a national monument.

SEVILLA PROVINCE

CARMONA

📧 😊😊😊 **Parador Alcázar del Rey Don Pedro,** tel. 954141010, fax 954143752. This newly renovated, one-of-a-kind knights' castle enjoys a commanding view of the Guadalquivir Valley.

🏛 **Roman excavations,** Tue-Fri 10 am-2 pm and 4-6 pm, Sat/Sun 10 am-2 pm.

ECIJA

❎ **Bodegón del Gallo,** C/ Arcipreste Aparicio 3, rustic restaurant serving classic regional cuisine.

SEVILLA

ℹ️ Mon-Fri 9:30 am-7:30 pm, Sat 9:30 am-2 pm, Av. de la Constitución 21 B, tel. 954221404 and Paseo de las Delicias 9, tel. 954234465.

📱 *AIRPORT:* Aeropuerto San Pablo, 12 km outside of town, tel. 954510677, airport bus leaves from Bar Iberia, C/ Almirante Lobo. *TRAIN STATION:* **Estación de Sta. Justa,** Av. Kansas City s/n, tel. 954414111. *BUS STATION:* **Estación Plaza de Armas,** Avda. del Cristo de Expiración. **Estación de Autobuses,** C/ Manuel Vázquez Sagastizabal s/n (at Prado San Sebastian), tel. 954417111. *CAR RENTALS:* **Budget,** Av. San Francisco Javier 9, Edificio Sevilla 2, tel. 954650703. **Triana Rent a Car,** C/ Pagés del Corro 159, tel. 954282979. **Sevilla Car,** C/ Almirante Lobo, Edificio Cristina, tel. 954222587. **Hertz,** airport and Av. Rep. Argentina 3, tel. 954514720, 954278887. **Avis,** airport and Av. de la Constitución 15, tel. 954514314 and 954216549. *RIDE SHARING:* C/ Gonzalez Cuadrado 49, tel. 94907852. *BOAT TRIPS* on the **Guadalquivir,** Cruceros Turisticos, boats leave from the dock at Torre del Oro, tel. 954561692.

📧 😊😊😊 **Hotel Alfonso XIII,** C/ San Fernando 2, tel. 954222850, fax 954216033. Live like a king in a luxury hotel with an Oriental touch. **Hacienda Benazuza,** Sanlúcar la Mayor, tel. 955703344, fax 955704310, a former estate, 15 minutes from Sevilla by car, has been transformed into an establishment that satisifies your greatest expectations. **Palacio del Alabardero,** C/ Zaragoza 20, tel. 954560637, fax 954563666. A former palace that still feels like one, with an excellent restaurant; has few rooms, so reserve early.

😊😊 **San Gil,** C/ Parra 28, tel. 954906811, fax 954906939. A hotel that abounds in charm, in the down-to-earth Macarena district. **Hotel Alvarez Quintero,** C/ Alvarez Quintero 9-13, tel. 954221298, fax 954564141, in a former villa.

😊 **Hostal Sierpes,** Corral del Rey 22, tel. 954224948, fax 954212107, pension in a historic villa, right in the center of town. **Hotel Murillo,** C/ Lope de Rueda 7-9, tel. 954216095, former palatial abode in the Santa Cruz district, air-conditioned. **Pensión Goya,** Mateos Gago 31, tel. 954211170, fax 954562988, small charming pension in the Santa Cruz district.

❎ **Casa Robles,** C/ Alvarez Quintero 58, popular eatery with atmosphere and terrific food. **Egaña Oriza,** C/ San Fernando 41, well-managed restaurant with top-notch Basque specialities. **San Marco,** C/ Cuna 6, the best of the Italian restaurants, in a former aristocratic abode dating from the 18th century. **Bodegón San Vicente,** C/ Tomás de Ybarra 2, only a few steps from the Cathedral, hearty food, good selection of tapas. **El Bacalao,** Pl. Ponce de León 15, a great place for stockfish fans. **Casa Antonio** and **Casa Manolo,** both on Plaza Alfalfa, folksy eateries, good prices.

TAPAS BARS: The locals customarily do a tapas bar crawl through a single district in one evening. Many bars offer an excellent selection of tapas, various appetizers that can easily take the place of dinner. The Triana district is an especially good place for tapas bars (C/ Betis, C/ San Jacinto, C/ de la Pureza), as are Arenall (C/ G. Vinuesa) and Santa Cruz (Pl. de los Venerables).

Giralda, C/ Mateos Gago 1, an establishment with a wide variety of tapas, always very crowded. **Bar Las Teresas,** C/ Sta. Teresa 2, loaded with atmosphere, guests clink glasses of sherry and consume ham tapas. **Bodega Morales,** C/ García Vinuesa, older than the hills, a Sevillan institution, in the lively Arenal district. **La Carbonería,** C/ Levies 18, bar with live music. **Café-Bar Abades,** C/ Abades 13, calm atmosphere, covered Andalusian patio. **Patio de San Eloy,** C/ San Eloy 18-20, extremely crowded – delicious tapas. **El Perejil,** Pl. San Jerónimo de Córdoba (near Hotel Don Paco). The sherry is served from pitchers and the owner entertains guests with passionate flamenco songs.

🎶 *FLAMENCO BARS:* **El Arenal,** C/ Rodo 7, tel. 954216492, performances daily 9 and 11:30 pm. **Los Gallos,** Pl. de Sta. Cruz 11, tel. 954216981.

🏛 **Museo de Bellas Artes,** Tue 3-8 pm, Wed-Sat 9 am-8 pm, Sun 9 am-3 pm, closed Mon and holidays. **Casa de Pilatos,** daily 9 am-7 pm. **Museo Arqueológico,** Tue 3-8 pm, Wed-Sat 9 am-2:30 pm, Sun 9 am-2:30 pm. **Museo de Arte Contemporaneo,** Tue-Sat 10 am-8 pm, Sun 10 am-2 pm. **Museo de Artes y Costumbres Populares,** Tue 3-8 pm, Wed-Sat 9 am-8 pm, Sun 10 am-3 pm. **Reales Alcázares,** Tue-Sat 9:30 am-7 pm, Sun 9:30 am-5 pm. **Casa Murillo,** Mon-Fri 10 am-1 pm and 4-7 pm, Sat/Sun 11 am-2 pm. **Cathedral** and **Giralda,** Mon-Sat 10:30 am-5 pm, Sun 2-6 pm. **Torre del Oro/Museo Naval,** Tue-Fri 10 am-2 pm, Sat/Sun 11 am-2 pm. **Archivo de las Indias,** Mon-Fri 10 am-1 pm. **Convento de Sta. Paula,** Tue-Sun 9 am-1 pm and 4:30-6:30 pm. **Basilica de la Macarena,** 9 am-

1 pm and 5-9 pm. **Iglesia del Salvador**, 6:30-9 pm. **Hospital de la Caridad**, Mon-Sat 10 am-1 pm and 3:30-6 pm. **Itálica** (outside town), Tue-Sat 9 am-8 pm Sun 10 am-3 pm.

✉ Avda. de la Constitución 32.
☎ Telefónica: Pl. de la Gavidia.
📷 **Bullfights**: Tickets, C/ Sierpes 50 A. **Isla Mágica** recreational park on the Expo '92 site, Mon-Thu 11 am-midnight, Fri-Sun 11 am-11 pm, tel. 902161716.

HUELVA PROVINCE

ARACENA
🏛 **Grutas de las Maravillas**, Mon-Fri 10:30 am-1:30 pm and 3-6 pm.

AYAMONTE
🛏 😊😊😊 **Parador Costa de la Luz**, El Castillito, tel 959320700, fax 959320700, an oasis of quiet, wonderful view of the Atlantic. 😊😊 **Don Diego**, C/ Ramón y Cajal, tel. 959470250, fax 959320250, children welcome here. 😊 **Marqués de Ayamonte**, Trajano 12, tel 959320126, basic, but neat and clean.

COTO DE DOÑANA
Reservations for Land Rover tours through the national park can be made at the El Acebuche visitor center, daily 8:30 am-7 pm, tel. 959430432.

HUELVA
ℹ Av. de Alemania. 12, tel. 959257403.
🛏 😊😊😊 **Luz Huelva**, Alameda Sundheim 26, tel. 959250011, fax 959258110, best hotel in the city. **Parador Cristóbal Colón**, Crta. Huelva-Matalascafias, km 24, tel. 959536300, fax 959536228, isolated coastal setting. 😊😊 **Hosteleria de la la Rábida**, tel 959350312, at the La Rábida monastery, good food in the adjoining restaurant.
🏛 **Museo Provincial**, Alameda Sundheim, Tue-Sat 9:30 am-2 pm and 4:30-7 pm (in summer 8:30 am-2:30 pm). **Monasterio de la Rábida** (outside town), Tue-Sun 10 am-1 pm and 4-6 pm.

MOGUER
🏛 **Santa Clara** monastery and museum, Tue-Sun 11 am-1 pm and 4:30-6:30 pm. **Museo Jiménez**, Tue-Sat 10 am-2 pm and 4:30-8 pm, Sun 10 am-2 pm.

RÍOTINTO
🏛 **Museo Minero**, daily 10 am-3 pm, mid-October to mid-May, Mon-Fri 10 am-3 pm, Sat/Sun and holidays 10 am-4 pm.

CÓRDOBA

ℹ **Palacio de Congresos y Exposiciónes de Córdoba**, C/ Torrijos 10, tel. 957471235.
🛏 😊😊😊 **Parador de Córdoba**, Av. de la Arruzafa,

tel. 957275900, fax 957280409, modern parador in an area with many villas, 20 minutes from town center. **Hespería C.**, Av. Confederación, tel. 957421042, fax 957299997, good location, great rooms. 😊😊 **Maimonides**, C/ Torrijos 4, tel. 957471500, fax 957483803, best of the three-stars, opposite the Mezquita. **Al Mihrab**, Apartado de Correos 760, tel./fax 957272198, hotel with a marvelous view of Córdoba. **González**, C/ Mariíquez 3, tel. 957479819, fax 957486187. 😊 **Maestre**, Romero Barros 4, tel. 957472410, fax 957475395, clean as a whistle, friendly staff. **Hostal Seneca**, C/ Conde y Luque 7, tel. 957473234, antiquated but romantic.
🍴 **El Caballo Rojo**, C/ Cardenal Herrero 26, excellent Hispano-Arabic cuisine. **Casa Pepe**, C/ Romero 1, the desserts are a knockout, best to reserve a table on the patio. **Bodega Casa de Campos**, C/ de los Lineros 32, traditional bodega where you drink sherry while seated amongst ancient kegs. **Taberna San Miguel**, Pl. San Miguel 3, old-fashioned, small, delicious tapas. **El Churrasco**, Romero 16, great meat from the charcoal grill. **Casa Rubio**, Puerta de Almodvar, tapas bar.
🏛 **Mosque / Cathedral**, Mon-Sat 10 am-7 pm, Sun and holidays 2-7 pm. **Alcázar de los Reyes Cristianos**, Mon-Sat 10 am-2 pm and 6-8 pm, Sun 9:30 am-3 pm. **Torre de la Calahorra**, daily 10 am-2 pm and 4:30-8:30 pm (winter 10 am-6 pm). Multimedia shows, 11 am, 12, 1, 3:30 and 4:30 pm. **Synagogue**, Tue-Sat 10 am-2 pm and 3:30-5:30 pm, Sun 10 am-1:30 pm. **Museo Arqueológico Provincial**, Pl. Jerónimo Páez, Tue 3-8 pm, Wed-Sat 9 am-8 pm, Sun 9 am-3 pm. **Museo Municipal Taurino** (bullfighting), Pl. de Maimónides, Tue-Sat 9:30 am-1:30 pm and 6-8 pm, Sun 9:30 am-3 pm. **Museo de Bellas Artes**, same hours as M. Arqueológico; **Museo Julio Romero de Torres**, Tue-Sun 10 am-2 pm and 5-7 pm, May-Sept. Tue-Sat 10 am-2 pm and 6-8 pm, Sun 9:30 am-3 pm. **Museo Diocesano de Bellas Artes**, C/ Torrijos 10, Mon-Fri 10:30 am-2 pm and 4-6:30 pm, Sat 10:30 am-2 pm, closed Sun/hol. **Museo Vivo Al-Andaluz**, daily 10 am-6 pm, May-Sept. daily 10 am-2 pm and 5:30-8:30 pm. **Palacio de los Marqueses de Viana**, Pl. de Don Gome 2, Tue-Thu 9 am-2 pm (winter Tue-Thu 10 am-1 pm and 4-6 pm). **Posada del Potro**, Sala de Cueros (handcrafted leather), Tue-Sat 9 am-2 pm and 6-8 pm, Sun 10 am-1:30 pm. **Medina Azahara**, palace of the caliphs, 8 km west of town, Tue-Sun 10 am-2 pm and 4-6:30 pm (summer Tue-Sat 6-8:30 pm), Sun and holidays 10 am-2 pm.
✉ C/ Cruz Conde 15.
🚆 *TRAIN STATION:* Avda. de América. RENFE office, Ronda de los Tejares 10. *BUS STATION:* Avda. de la Victoria.

JAÉN
Land of Olives

Olive groves extend as far as the eye can see across the gentle rolling hills of the province of Jaén, lending a seductive charm to this region, which is geographically differentiated from the Castilian plateau to the north by the intervening Sierra Morena mountains.

The provincial capital of **Jaén** ⓸ (population 112,000) is the commercial hub of the world's largest olive-growing region. Its name derives from the Arabic *geén,* which means "caravan station." While Jaén's geographical location at the intersection of the border between Andalusia and Castile has historically been a boon to trade, it has also repeatedly brought bloody conflicts to the province, among them the Battle of Las Navas de Tolosa

(1212), as a result of which Alfonso VIII of Castile wrested control of much of Andalusia from the Moors; and Napoleon's first defeat in the famous Battle of Bailén (1808).

The formidable outline of the fortress of **Santa Catalina**, now restored and serving as the regional parador, looms above the city it once protected. In the working-class district of **Barrio de la Magdalena** at the foot of the Sierra de Jabalcuz are the underground ★**Baños Arabes**. Their size (470 square meters) and excellent state of preservation make them one of the most noteworthy and interesting examples of Arab baths in Spain. The **Palacio de Villadompardo** and its folk art museum, the **Museo de Artes y Costumbres Populares**, are located right above the baths. The magnificent ★**Cathedral**, with its Baroque façade, stands out in Jaén's otherwise rather prosaic cityscape. The masterpiece of the great Andalusian architect Andrés de Vandelvira, construction on the edifice was begun in 1500. Its most significant

Above: Olive groves predominate in the landscape of the province of Jaén. Right: A test of strength against bulls in the streets of Torreperogil near Úbeda.

Map pp. 14-15, Info p. 73

relic is the sudarium of St. Veronica, which is shown to worshipers every Friday after mass.

The **Museo Provinical** is in the modern section of Jaén. In addition to a picture gallery, it contains archaeological finds, among them a superb Iberian statue known as "The Bull of Porcuna."

Baeza and Úbeda – Renaissance Pure and Simple

A trip northeastwards from Jaén to the fairy-tale Renaissance villages of Baeza and Úbeda leads past oceans of olive groves. The two communities, which are only 10 kilometers apart, were important outposts during the reconquest of Andalusia, as well as thriving commercial centers on the Castilian border. **★Baeza 43** was also home to both a university and a bishopric for a time. At the entrance to the latter, the visitor is struck by the small but sublime **Plaza del Pópulo**, with its lion-studded fountain and statue of Hannibal's wife Imilce. In the 16th century, various buildings were erected on the square, including the slaughterhouse and the **Casa del Pópulo** (Court of Appeals). The arches of Puerta de Jaén and Arco de Villarlar were erected in honor of Charles V, the former in 1526 to celebrate his betrothal, and the latter after he quelled the revolt of the Castilian cities (*comuneros*).

Dreamy strolls on the **Paseo de las Murallas** overlooking the Guadalquivir Valley inspired the romantic and introspective poetry of Antonio Machado, who taught at the university here from 1912 to 1919. Baeza being a farming town, the following bucolic story is often told: When Machado arrived and asked for the rector, he was told that the latter was "in agony." "Good Lord!" Machado exclaimed, but calmed down when the locals informed him that "Agony" was in fact the name of a bar for farmhands. Such bars still exist today, providing farmhands with a forum in which to air their grievances against bad harvests and the weather.

Plaza Santa María recalls the greatness that was 16th-century Baeza. A wide staircase leads up to the mighty Renaissance **Cathedral**. The side portal, Puerta de la Luna, is built in Gothic Mudéjar style. An impressive Baroque monstrance is housed inside the building. On a small square below the Cathedral is the Romanesque church of **Santa Cruz**, with its twin pointed portals; the Isabelline **Palacio del Marqués de Jabalquinto**, with its elaborately decorated façade, a Renaissance inner courtyard and a Baroque staircase; and the old **University** (now a public school and in the summer a venue for university courses), which bears a Mannerist façade. The **Town Hall** is noteworthy as well, the splendor of its exterior belying the fact that it originally served as a prison.

★**Úbeda** ⓭, a hymn of praise to the Renaissance, is an inferno in summer and bleak and cold in winter. It is difficult to single out only one of the town's sights: countless palaces and magnificent squares give visitors the feeling of having stumbled upon an outdoor museum of the Renaissance.

At the edge of town is the Mannerist **Hospital de Santiago**, comprised of a church and a two-story arcaded courtyard. **Plaza de Santa Maria** was laid out by the well-heeled De los Cobos family, while the church of ★**San Salvador** by Vandelvira and Diego de Siloe was erected as a mausoleum for Don Francisco de los Cobos, secretary to Charles V. The palace next door, which is now a **Parador**, began life as a humble parsonage. At the other end of the square is the **Town Hall**, which sports a neoclassical façade. The church of **Santa Maria** across the way was built on the foundations of a mosque. A little higher up you encounter the market square, with the Gothic church of **San Pablo** and the **Old Town Hall**.

A short distance away is the 17th-century **Oratorio de San Juan de la**

Above: A vulture shades her young in the nest (Sierra de Cazorla y Segura).

Cruz, which was built over the very place where the eponymous mystic departed this world in 1591. His mortal remains are inside.

**Parque Natural de Cazorla y Segura – Andalusia's Green Oasis

The jumping-off point for the national park surrounding it, the charming town of *Cazorla ⑮, guarded by two fortresses, nestles in the foothills of the Cazorla and Segura ranges, whose outlines are visible from a great distance. The church of **Santa María** attests to both the depredations of the Napoleonic era and (once again) the genius of Andrés de Vandelvira.

La Iruela, whose fortress is the extension of a sharp crag, is the gateway to the **Sierra de Cazorla y Segura** national park. The park's mountainous landscape, with peaks reaching 2,000 meters, contains vast forests of holm, silver fir, larch and ash (the latter now rare in Andalusia). In spring such botanical delights as the Cazorla violet flourish. The park's remote location makes it an ideal refuge for wild boar, mouflons (a type of wild sheep), eagles, falcons and deer. The Guadalquivir, Andalusia's largest river, rises in the nearby mountains. A challenging footpath leads to **Cañada de las Fuentes**, the source of the Guadalquivir River. At the Vadillo sawmill, an aerobically undemanding path leads to "Devil's Falls," and another good walking path winds along the Borosa River. The information center, **Torre de Vinagre**, can be found by heading towards the Embalse del Tranco (a dam), where the Museo de Ciencias Naturales (Museum of Natural History) and a small Jardín Botánico are also located. Just before the dam is the **Parque Cinegetico**, a game reserve where, like an enchanted castle, the Arab fortress at Bujaraiza rises out of the waters which swallowed up the eponymous village.

JAÉN PROVINCE

BAEZA
i Plaza del Pópulo, tel. 953740444.
🛏 ⊖⊖⊖ **Hotel Juanito**, Paseo Arco del Agua, s/n, tel. 953740040, fax 953742324, sensibly furnished hotel with a restaurant renowned throughout the province for its fine cuisine.
✖ **Casa Juanito**, Paseo Arca del Agua, tel. 953740040, considered to be the best restaurant in the city.
🏛 **Cathedral**, daily 10 am-1 pm and 4-6 pm.

CAZORLA
🛏 ⊖⊖⊖ **Parador El Adelantado**, Sierra de Cazorla, tel. 953721075, fax 953721077, well-run modern parador in a lovely setting.
⊖⊖ **Noguera de la Sierpe**, Coto Rios, tel. 953713021, fax 953713109, rustic atmosphere, restaurant serves tasty game dishes.
📩 Information regarding **Sierra de Cazorla** national park: Oficina del Parque Natural, Cazorla, C/ Martinez Falero 11, tel. 953720115, and at the information center Torre del Vinagre, Carretera de Tranco, km 18. **Museo de Ciencias Naturales** and **Jardín Botánico**, Tue-Sun 11 am-2 pm and 5-8 pm.

JAÉN
i Arquitecto Berges 1, tel. 953222737.
🛏 ⊖⊖⊖ **Parador Castillo de Santa Catalina**, tel. 953230000, fax 953230930, this unique knight's castle has been converted into a tranquil hotel with a now famous restaurant that provides diners with a breathtaking view along with the great food.
⊖⊖ **Rey Fernando**, Pl. de Coca de la Pifiera 7, tel. 953251840, nice clean hotel.
🏛 **Cathedral**, daily 8:30 am-1 pm and 4:30-7 pm, museum only Sat/Sun 11 am-1 pm. **Baños Árabes** in the **Palacio de Villardompardo** with **Museo de Artes y Costumbres Populares**, Tue 3-8 pm, Wed-Sat 9 am-8 pm, Sun 9 am-3 pm. **San Ildefonso**, daily 8 am-12 pm and 6-9 pm. **Castillo de Santa Catalina**, Tue-Thu 10:30 am-1:30 pm.
📱 *BUS STATION:* Plaza de la Coca de la Pinera.

ÚBEDA
i Plaza de los Caidos, s/n, tel. 953750897.
🛏 ⊖⊖⊖ **Parador Condestable Divalos**, P1 Vázquez de Molina 1, tel. 953750345, fax 953751259, delightfully tranquil parador with an elegant restaurant and good cafeteria on the patio.
⊖⊖ **Consuelo**, C/ Ramón y Cajal 12, tel. 953-750840, fax 953756834, good, solid traditional fare.

Andalusia

SHERRY

North of the Bay of Cádiz just slightly above sea level lies the wine-growing region of Jerez. In this triangular area delimited by the cities of Sanlúcar de Barrameda, Puerto de Santa María and Jerez de la Frontera the best-tasting and most illustrious of Spanish wines are produced. Proximity to the sea, the combined blessings of many long sunny days and fairly abundant rainfall, as well as the white spongy *alberiza* soil that soaks up water and at the same time reflects the sunlight onto the grapes from the ground below – these conditions make the "Sherry Triangle" ideal for the production of wines of superior quality. Most of the grapes grown here are of the Palomino Fino variety.

Sherry production involves a unique process. The wine is stored in the *bodegas*

Above: A sherry bodega in Chiclana. Right: Spaniards always have a little something to eat while they drink – tapas.

in long rows of oak barrels that are stacked three to seven tiers high, with the oldest wine, the *solera,* in the lower tiers. From time to time wine is drawn off from the solera (no more than one third), after which wine from the next highest *criadera* tier is drawn down in its place. The wine must pass through up to six criaderas before it is considered properly aged. The barrels are never emptied. The year in which the solera began is the "age" that appears on the bottle. The minimum age is three years.

This process, together with the vintners' long years of experience, fosters the production of wines whose quality is not in any way affected by climactic variations from one year to the other. The quantity of wine produced does fluctuate, however, reaching between one and two million hectoliters annually.

The microorganism content of the wine is another crucial aspect of sherry viniculture. During their first year of storage, some wines grow a mildew-like substance called *flor* before the solera pro-

cess described above begins. These wines are classified as *Fino.*

The principal types of sherry are *Fino:* 15-17 percent alcohol, pale and rather dry; *Amontillado:* 16-18 percent alcohol, but 24 percent if allowed to mature longer at the must stage, darker and with a somewhat nutty flavor; *Oloroso*: 18-20 percent, golden in color, somewhat heavier flavor; *Cream*: made from overripe grapes, fairly sweet, similar to Oloroso; *Moscatel:* rich, sweet, made from muscat raisins; *Manzanilla,* a word which in common usage means chamomile, but in this context is the name for the *Finos* from Sanlúcar, which are very dry and somewhat tart.

Thirteen villages in all grow grapes especially for sherry production or "raising," as it is called. But the wines from **Condado** (Niebla, Huelva Province), **Chiclana** and **Montilla-Moriles** (Córdoba Province) are made by the same solera process, although the Montilla wines are produced from a different kind of grapes (Pedro Ximénez).

The history of the Jerez wines has been documented as far back as Phoenician times. In 1588, the English took a supply with them to Plymouth, in which setting Shakespeare has Falstaff praise "Jerez" in *Henry IV.* Shakespeare called it sherry, which sounded similar to the Arabic name for the town, and at the same time was easier for English speakers to pronounce. The English entered the sherry business in the 19th century when such concerns as Sandeman, Croft, Williams and Humbert, Terry, Osborne and Garvey began channeling capital into this lucrative business.

The vintners use special long-stemmed wine-tasting goblets called *venencias* to draw off samples of the wine in order to check the progress of the maturation process. Sherry glasses are traditionally narrow in order to preserve the bouquet. Bars located in the sherry triangle rarely serve any other kind of wine but sherry. Although sherry is not a table wine, a glass or two of ice-cold *Fino* can make a delicious *tapa* taste even better.

FLAMENCO

Flamenco music is made up of a synergy of poetry, music and rhythm. These three elements are used to express the most profound human emotions – joy, hate and hope; passion, jealousy and fear. Lyrics and music are fused, like ice to metal. Flamenco singing, which sounds as though it were wrenched from the soul, is known as *cantejondo* – best translated perhaps as "fervent singing."

The guitar has been the instrumental accompaniment for flamenco since the 19th century, although the instrument has never truly achieved the status of a full partner, remaining instead a complement to the song within the framework of a dialogue between singer and guitar. However, some songs such as the ancient *tonás* and *trilleras* are traditionally performed without instrumental accompani-

Above and Right: Flamenco dancing has different expressions – sometimes restrained, sometimes passionate.

ment. Rhythm is particularly important in the *de compás* songs, and the audience sometimes claps in time to the music, especially at song festivals.

Although song is closely linked with flamenco, flamenco dance is also an art form in its own right. It has also become fashionable in recent years, primarily owing to Carlos Saura's film *Carmen* (1983), which caused a sensation and won flamenco innumerable new devotees worldwide. A number of flamenco academies also exist.

The first known use of the term *flamenco* is in early 19th century Andalusian folklore. In 18th-century argot the word meant braggart or show-off, and in Andalusia it referred to the gypsies.

The gypsies had come to the western part of Andalusia in the 15th century. Although they had gradually managed to adapt to regional mores, like agricultural day laborers and Moriscos they were still treated as outsiders. Yet little by little they fused their own musical modalities with those of Andalusian folk music, and it was this process that gave birth to flamenco song, which also drew upon Arabic, Jewish, Gregorian and Byzantine musical traditions.

Flamenco song, originally an informal, highly personal form of expression, only gradually evolved into a performance art suitable for public consumption. The first flamenco singer of renown, the legendary Tío (Uncle) Luís, emerged at the end of the 18th century. He was followed by such colorful performers as El Planeta, Franco el Colorao, El Fillo and La Perla, all of whom laid the groundwork for what would become the flamenco tradition.

The end of the 19th century saw the advent of the great gypsy singers who perfected flamenco style: Mara Borrico, Enrique El Mellizo, Loco Mateo, Diego el Marrurro and Joaquín el de la Paula, as well as the non-gypsy Silverio Franconetti, a key figure who was born in Sevilla in 1830 and was the founder of the *cafés cantantes.* Famous performers in the early 20th century included Manuel Torre, Tomás Pavón and Pastora Pavón, the latter known as *La Niña de los Peines* (The Girl of the Combs).

In the latter half of the 19th century, flamenco expanded beyond the intimacy of the small gatherings of devotees that had characterized the Andalusian gypsy environment, and began a process of "coming out" in flamenco bars. The first of these was opened in Sevilla in 1842, but without a doubt the most famous was Silverio Franconetti's, which opened in 1885. *Cafés cantates* soon sprung up in Madrid as well, and some became famous. They attracted a clientele that wanted first and foremost to have a good time, and there is disagreement to this day as to whether or not the growth of flamenco was beneficial to its purity of style. Be that as it may, the audiences consisted of a kaleidoscopic cross-section of Spanish society: the rich, the toreros, the aristocracy and the working class were all well represented.

In the 20th century, flamenco went out of fashion and the cafés cantates gradually disappeared. Manuel de Falla, aided by other intellectuals like García Lorca, organized a flamenco song competition in Granada to see if the form could be rescued from oblivion, but they met with little success. Competitions were again held in the 1950s, and this time the results were much more encouraging. The national flamenco competition in Córdoba in 1956 generated a groundswell of popular enthusiasm. Antonio Alcor deserves a great deal of credit for collecting traditional flamenco songs in the 1950s and helping the general public to acquire a taste for flamenco.

Modern-day flamenco has numerous admirers, most of whom belong to organizations known as *peñas flamencas*, which support flamenco artists, carry out research on flamenco styles and try to spread the gospel of flamenco. Among

the more prominent peñas are the Peña Juan Breva in Málaga and the Peña de la Plantería in Granada. Every last little village in Andalusia now has its peña. And in Madrid in recent years, flamenco has become increasinaly fashionable among the chic set, who take *Sevillana* courses and at festivals display what they consider to be southern exuberance by means of certain meticulously rehearsed quicksteps and exaggerated twists of the wrist. Intellectuals have also rediscovered flamenco. Musicologists study its various forms, publish anthologies and compendiums, and supervise new releases of old recordings.

The heart of flamenco has always beaten most strongly in western Andalusia. But Madrileños have also contributed to the popularity of flamenco by attending performances given by the best-known Andalusian artists at flamenco clubs. Flamenco is now known virtually everywhere, and there are experts in this art form in Paris, London, New York and Tokyo.

FIESTAS

There is no Spanish town without its fiesta, and no fiesta without *verbena* (partying) on the village square, the annual fair with wine, High Mass, parades, fireworks and above all bullfights. The whole village hums with energy. Suddenly everyone is in a good mood and just wants to enjoy the music – and nobody feels like working. The bars are overflowing, and hordes of children careen through the streets. For visitors to Spain, a village festival is the perfect pretext for a side-trip; a unique opportunity to mingle with the locals and at the same time take part in the festivities.

Bullfighting

Bullfighting is an integral part of every fiesta, even if all Spaniards don't approve

Above: Picadores provoke the bull with their lances. Right: The cuadrillas parade into the stadium before the bullfight – the paseillo.

of certain aspects of the spectacle. Many find the sport gruesome, others simply find it boring. There are people, some of them active members of animal rights organizations, who find it immoral in a civilized country to turn the killing of bulls into a celebratory national pastime. Yet, the fact remains – the relatively high price of tickets notwithstanding – that bullfights consistently sell out and that for most villagers a fiesta just isn't a fiesta without a *corrida de toros*.

Bullfighting has deep roots in Spanish culture. The first historical evidence of the existence of bullfighting antedates both the "bull games" on Crete and the Roman circus, where the bull was grabbed by the horns and wrestled to the ground. Figures representing bulls have been found at all prehistoric sites. In medieval times, numerous legends centered around bulls, and some Spanish plays from the Golden Age contain bullfighting scenes.

Bullfighting in its present-day form is essentially an 18th-century folklore spec-

tacle. Prior to this time, it was a sport practiced by noblemen on horseback. But under the Bourbons it fell out of favor among the aristocracy, and this gave the common people the opportunity to explore its own enthusiasm for a previously forbidden pleasure. It was they who originated the practice of doing battle with the bull on foot; horses having been relegated to the performance of minor tasks for the picadors. The increasing popularity of this form of bullfighting was accompanied by the advent of the first professional toreros (some of whose names became the 18th-century equivalents of today's pop stars), as well as the first arenas built specifically for bullfighting. The oldest surviving arena, in Ronda, dates back to 1785 and is still in use today.

During this period, two different forms of bullfighting were competing for supremacy. The Ronda style, most famously practiced by Pedro Romero, was precise and restrained, while the more spontaneous and lively Sevilla style was linked with the torero Pepe Hillo.

The first great bullfighters introduced the practice of dividing the corrida into three tercios, and developed various techniques the torero could use to trick the bull. They also perfected the art of the death blow. Pepe Hillo wrote *Tauromaquia*, or "The Art of Bullfighting," which set forth the principles of bullfighting. Jesulin de Ubrique has made a name for herself with bullfighting for women only.

Numerous artists have used bullfighting as a theme in their work. One of the first to do so was Goya. He created a series of etchings entitled *Tauromaquia* immortalizing famous bullfighters (among them his good friend Martincho), and depicted in reportorial detail the death in the arena of the torero Pepe Hillo. Picasso produced a famous series of bullfighting paintings that were inspired by Goya's *Tauromaquia*.

Some 60,000 bulls or *novillos* (young bulls) are killed in the arena each year. Of the approximately 500 toreros active at any one time, a maximum of 20 ever

achieve popularity. Naturally, every tore-ro dreams of becoming a star, of being greeted by thousands upon thousands of white handkerchiefs (which is how spectators demonstrate their affection for a matador). Toreros traditionally come from farming villages, where many young men regard bullfighting as an exciting and upwardly mobile escape from their humble origins.

Nowadays there are schools for aspiring bullfighters. But in the past, budding bullfighters were forced to find an estate that bred *toros bravos* (wild fighting bulls) and sneak over the fence under cover of darkness. This was, and remains, an autodidactic pursuit fraught with danger, as the bulls are closely watched.

Matadors trying to make the big time travel a long, slow road from bullfights in temporary arenas at village festivals, to

Above: The matador provokes the already weakened bull with his muleta (red cape).
Right: Procession of penitents during Semana Santa.

seeing their names in small print on large posters, to top billing in a big city arena. It can take years before an agent discovers a talented young bullfighter and takes him under his wing, and many young matadors end up languishing in obscurity. The ones who do get a lucky break begin as *novilleros.* Having demonstrated possession of the right stuff, they are issued a license by a *diestro* (an experienced torero) authorizing them to practice the profession of matador. This means they may only fight large bulls (over 450 kilos) in arenas of the first rank.

A good *diestro* earns between one and five million pesetas per corrida, in the course of which he dispatches two bulls. A total of three matadors and six bulls appear in each corrida. Illustrious matadors usually retire at about 40, having accumulated enough money to go into the bull breeding business – or having grown weary of making a career of flirting with death. The risk of death faced by bullfighters has given rise to a vast literature on their demise, the best-known poem on this theme being Federico García Lorca's *At Five O'clock in the Afternoon,* a lament on the death of the then-renowned matador Sanchez Mejías.

Various Festivals

In Cádiz ★★*Carnival* is celebrated by one and all. Every carnival concludes with the "burial of the sardines" parade and funeral procession of the "widows." These events also mark the beginning of the annual round of fiestas which are celebrated in every Spanish village on their respective patron saint's feast day. The festivals most widely celebrated are San Juan (June 25), San Pedro (June 29), Santiago (July 25), the Virgin del Carmen (July 16), the Assumption (August 15) and the Feast of the Suffering Virgin (September 15).

Easter Week, ★★*Semana Santa, is* steeped in tradition in Andalusia as well. Folkloric artworks called *pasos* are carried through the streets in the processions. Individuals can, if the spirit moves them, sing a *saeta,* which brings the entire procession to a reverent halt. In such cities as ★★Sevilla and Málaga, Semana Santa is a major festival whose religious character doesn't prevent bars from staying open all night. Processions in smaller villages (e.g., Úbeda, ★★Ronda, Baena, Puente Genil and Jerez de los Caballeros) also have surprises in store for visitors.

Andalusian Ferias: The Andalusian *ferias* are not religious in nature. Well before the summer heat sets in and while the orange trees are still in bloom, Sevillans throng the streets of their city. The ★★*Feria de Abril* begins two weeks after Easter, and sometimes earlier. This *feria* is an intensely colorful blend of horses, costumes, wine, music and dance. The festival area is packed with *casetas* (tents) set up by various clubs or organizations which outfit their area with a bar, tables and a dance floor. The annual fair adjoins the tent area. The horse show takes place

in the morning, and the afternoon is reserved for family events. Dancing, which continues through the night, follows. Ferias follow pretty much the same format everywhere, but the ones in small towns are sometimes more spontaneous.

The second-largest is the ★★*Feria del Caballo,* which features Jerez horses. Particularly appealing are the ferias in the environs of Cádiz, Puerto de Santa María, Puerto Real, Rota and Chipiona.

The dates of the various ferias are determined by the church calendar. Whitsun is the day for the *Feria de la Manzanilla* in Sanlúcar, where in summer horse races are also held on the beach on Sundays. The Jerez grape harvest festival in September marks the end of the yearly round of celebrations.

The Andalusian pilgrimages are often rooted in ancient folk superstitions. García Lorca set his play *Yerma* against the backdrop of the *El Cristo del Paño* pilgrimage in Moclín (Granada, October 1). Other Andalusian festivals include the *Cascamorras* in Baza and Guadix (Sep-

tember 6), which harks back to an ancient enmity between the two towns. Córdobans celebrate the *Fiesta de los Patios* by decorating their courtyards. Granada holds a colorful ★*Fiesta de las Cruces* in early May.

El Rocío

The Virgin of ★★*El Rocío* attracts over one million people annually to the Whitsunday pilgrimage in her honor. The biggest folkloric festival in Andalusia (and perhaps in Spain) lasts three days and is held in an area that's as flat as a pancake and virtually devoid of restaurants, hotels, inns or restrooms. An event that at first glance looks like a jumble of people, horses, ox-drawn wagons and wine is in fact organized around strict protocols which even assign a specific role to tourists. As recently as 1959, there wasn't so

Above: Young and old don their finery for the fiesta. Right: In Granada, decorated ox carts depart for the pilgrimage to El Rocio.

much as a paved road to El Rocío, which lent the event an incomparably folkloric atmosphere. Today's festival is attended by over 70 brotherhoods from throughout Andalusia, plus one group each from Madrid and Barcelona, a group of Spaniards living abroad and literally hordes of onlookers.

The statue of the Virgin venerated here dates back to the 13th century, although the pilgrimage itself is "only" two centuries old. The pilgrimage chapel and buildings around it were erected in the 20th century, and increasing numbers of amenities for tourists have sprung up around them in recent years.

The *hermandades* (brotherhoods) organize the pilgrimage according to rituals and traditions that have been handed down through the generations. They travel by ox-drawn wagon from throughout Andalusia, and are often on the road for up to three or four days. Like settlers in an epic Western, they arrive in columns of white covered wagons, bringing with them their wives and children and a week's worth of provisions and kitchen utensils, plus food and blankets for their horses and oxen. In recent years, the oxen have increasingly been supplanted by tractors and off-road vehicles, alongside of which the men ride their noble Andalusian steeds. Their route takes them over gravel and dirt tracks, and they are granted special permission to cut through the Coto de Doñana National Park. Each column has one *simpecado*, a wagon more ornately decorated than the others in which a tiny shrine and the brotherhood's banner are kept.

By Friday evening all participants have made their way to within three kilometers of the pilgrims' chapel. A detachment is then sent out during the night to prepare the accommodations for the various brotherhoods. Finally, on Saturday morning, the gaily decorated wagons make their way to the chapel to greet the Virgin. The festivities rollick on for hours, complete with music, *vino fino,* songs and solemn dances performed on the beach, the *Sevillanas Rocieras.*

Mass is said on Sunday morning as automobile-borne city dwellers pour into town, jostling each other to be near the Virgin and in some cases succumbing to fits of religious ecstasy upon entering the chapel. That night, rosaries are said and a procession is held, during which the participants sing *Ave Marias* as they pay their respects to the *hermandades* at their respective lodgings. The day ends with a fireworks display and yet another festive celebration.

On Whitmonday, the grand procession begins at the crack of dawn. To the young men from the Almonte *hermandad* of the Rocío community belong the exclusive honor and privilege of carrying the Virgin in the procession. People are packed in so tightly that the Virgin is rocked back and forth as if she were riding on a ship ploughing through roiling waves. If a non-Almonte should venture too close to the Virgin, they are summarily adminis-

tered a merciless drubbing. But people keep trying to get as close as possible to the venerated figure, if only for a fleeting moment. The procession stops at each of the fraternal houses and sings a *Salve Regina*. The conclusion of this procession in the scorching midday heat marks the official end of the festivities.

When the exhausted and hung-over retinues of pilgrims arrive back in their home towns they are given a tumultuous welcome, which revives their spirits – and the singing and dancing begins all over again.

The Rocío is now a televised national spectacle that goes on and on like a carnival parade. After all, it takes money, and lots of it, to buy luxurious horses and costumes, and to be able to take a week off work into the bargain. The less privileged stand by the roadside selling soft drinks and worthless trinkets. The Rocío pilgrimage is indeed a religious occasion, but for the brotherhoods who make it happen, it also provides an opportunity for them to show off.

FROM KITCHEN AND WINE CELLAR

In Spain, country inns, picnic areas, gourmet restaurants and the neighborhood bar all have one thing in common: they are habitually packed with people who are laughing, talking and enjoying food and drink together. There's no two ways about it: the Spanish are dyed-in-the-wool epicureans. Good food and drink don't just keep body and soul together – they make life worth living.

From a culinary standpoint, the day gets off to a slow, even spartan start: A wake-up *café solo* (espresso), *café cortado* (espresso with a dash of milk) or *cqfé con leche* (coffee with plenty of milk), preferably consumed standing in a bar on the way to work. The *café* isn't completely solo, though: a piece of cake, or a croissant or, for a change of pace,

Above: Appetizingly presented – seafood in a specialty restaurant. Right. Paella, the best-known Spanish rice dish.

churros (fritters) dipped in hot chocolate accompany the warm wake-up beverage.

Next, at 2 p.m. comes lunch. Traditionally, the midday meal, a substantial and elaborate one, is eaten in the bosom of the family. But work-related pressures are making lighter meals the rule during the *siesta*. The traditional but time-consuming cooking and eating orgies are increasingly relegated to weekends or holidays, of which Spain has plenty.

Outposts of fast-food chains are now, for better or worse, a relatively common sight in Spain, and all the more so in tourist areas. Fortunately for the health of the nation, however, the Spanish have developed *tapas*, a versatile and delicious alternative to burgers and fries. These appetizers were invented in Andalusia, where a *tapa* (cover) originally designated a glass cover that prevented insects from flying into your sherry glass. Tapas culture from the deep south of Spain took the rest of the nation by culinary storm: what better way to spend an evening than to go from bar to bar, drinking and snack-

Kitchen and Wine Cellar

ing, until the tourists have abandoned their restaurant tables and the Spaniards themselves can have dinner; which they rarely do before 9 p.m.

Andalusia has always been regarded as Spain's "poorhouse" – and this is reflected in the low-cost, filling and imaginatively prepared fare on the region's menus. However, a goodly number of "poor people's" dishes that have been retooled by savvy chefs can be found today on the menus of fine restaurants – including gazpacho, a cold and refreshing vegetable soup.

Olives play an indispensable role here – no great surprise in view of the fact that the province of Jaén is the largest olive-growing region in Europe. Olive oil is used for frying or is drizzled on bread, while countless varieties of olives please the palates of tapas lovers.

When it comes to seafood, the Andalusians have a predilection for *pescaito frito* (fried fish). And, consistent with their love of bullfighting, *rabo de toro* (bull's tail) is another favorite dish.

About *jamon* volumes could be written. The costliest and best-known varieties of this mountain-cured ham come from Jabugo in the Sierra de Aracena (Iberico) and Trevelez in the Alpujarras (Serrano). Its fine flavor stems from the half-wild Iberian pigs fed on grass, herbs and acorns.

The seemingly infinite realm of tapas extends from shrimp and fish, *chorizo* (spicy sausage) and ham to flavorful stuffed vegetables and carefully composed salads. Typical Andalusian variations include *riñones al Jerez* (kidneys in sherry). A favorite tapa among many Spaniards is *tortilla española* (potato omelet). The beverage customarily served with tapas is *Fino* (dry sherry). The sweet version is served with desserts.

The Arabs introduced almond trees into Spain, which blossom into a sea of white in January and February. In the kitchen the tasty nuts are used not only as a binder in sauces but also as the main ingredient in cakes, cookies, marzipan and *turrón* (white nougat).

METRIC CONVERSION

Metric Unit	US Equivalent
Meter (m)	39.37 in.
Kilometer (km)	0.6241 mi.
Square Meter (sq m)	10.76 sq. ft.
Hectare (ha)	2.471 acres
Square Kilometer (sq km)	0.386 sq. mi.
Kilogram (kg)	2.2 lbs.
Liter (l)	1.05 qt.

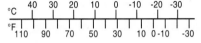

TRAVEL PREPARATIONS

Climate

Average temperatures in May, July and September; daily high in August (°C):

	May	July	Sept	Aug
Almería	19	25	24	38
Granada	17	26	22	40
Málaga	19	25	23	38
Cádiz	19	24	23	42
Sevilla	20	27	24	45
Córdoba	20	27	24	45

Inland, temperatures tend to be higher in the middle of the day and somewhat lower at night than these averages indicate. On the more humid coast, temperature fluctuations are less extreme and nights warmer than in inland regions. Although typical Mediterranean summer weather can be counted on in July and August, the best months to travel from a climactic standpoint are May, June, September and October, though the weather is more fickle during these periods than in summer. Rain gear and a warm sweater or jacket are a must in mountainous regions and on the northern coast.

Currency

The Spanish *peseta* has been a relatively stable currency since Spain joined the EU. Bring along travelers checks or internationally accepted credit cards. You will always need your passport or national identity card when changing money. Many banks with *Cambio* (exchange) signs do not accept Eurochecks.

Exchange offices advertise good rates but often charge large commissions. Most larger hotels will change money for their guests without charges. Bank cards from other European countries can be used at many automatic tellers.

There are 1,000, 2,000, 5,000 and 10,000 peseta notes, and occasionally 500 peseta notes, too. Coins are 1, 5, 10, 25, 50, 100, 200 and 500 pesetas. As of 1997 the old coins with Franco on them are no longer valid.

Exchange Rates:

US $1	. . . .	161 ESP
CAN $1	. . . .	109 ESP
UK £1	. . . .	261 ESP
AUS $1	. . . .	102 ESP

Health

No vaccinations are required. You can drink the water in Spain everywhere; even from public fountains.

Arrival / Customs

Members of European Union countries can enter Spain with their identity card or passport. Visitors from non-EU countries need a valid passport.

For private travel within the EU, goods for personal use can be brought in without limitations, with the exception of luxuries for which the following limits apply: 800 cigarettes, 400 cigarillos, 200 cigars, 1 kg of tobacco; 10 liters of spirits, 20 liters of other alcoholic beverages with a maximum alcohol content of 22 percent, 90 liters of wine (of which a maximum of 60 liters of sparkling wine is allowed), 110 liters of beer.

Visitors from non-EU countries may bring with them up to 10 kg of foodstuffs and non-alcoholic beverages, 200 cigarettes or 250 grams of tobacco, 1 liter of spirits or 2 liters of wine. The same limits apply to goods purchased in duty-free shops of non-EU countries, as well as for goods purchased within Spain in a duty-free shop. As of 1999, duty-free shopping is no longer possible for those traveling within the EU free-trade zone (e.g., from the UK to Spain).

TRAVELING TO ANDALUSIA

The most convenient way to get to Andalusia is by air, as the region's public transportation system is far from state-of-the-art. For predominantly urban vacations, flying is definitely the best bet, and for side-trips, rental cars are available.

TRAVELING IN ANDALUSIA

By Car
There are national roads, regional roads and streets within towns and villages. Conditions are usually quite good on all of them. *Autopistas* (freeways) are subject to tolls (*peaje*), and unlike *autovias*, where you pay nothing, lightly traveled and devoid of delays arising from traffic jams. Major credit cards (Mastercard and Visa) and EC cards are accepted on toll roads.

By Bicycle
It is becoming more and more popular to travel around Europe by bike, but note that a high percentage of Spain is as mountainous as Switzerland! There are no bicycle routes, but there are many seldom-used provincial roads. Arriving by train with a bike is possible, although not on all trains. This variation is still better than taking your bike in the car, because you should never park and leave a packed car in Spain. Most airlines now allow for the shipment of bikes, for which they generally charge a fixed rate.

By Plane
Iberia, the Spanish national airline, offers flights from Madrid and Barcelona to 20 destinations within Spain (in Andalusia: Almería, Granada, Málaga, Jerez de la Frontera and Sevilla). Additional domestic flights are offered by Aviaco, Air Europa, Spanair and other smaller airlines. Lower fares are sometimes available from these carriers.

By Train
Spain's railway connections suffer from the ageing broad-gauge railway tracks and the many mountains. The network does not cover all parts of the country and is not well served.

There are three categories of long distance trains: *Interurbano, Talgo* and *Express*. The latter cost more. A high-speed train, the *AVE*, connects Madrid and Sevilla some 20 times daily in about three hours. The railway companies are *Renfe* and *Feve*. Tickets for longer journeys should be bought with seat reservations in advance. There are special offers on weekends on journeys from Madrid, the so-called *trenes lince*, cheap round-trip tickets, to Jaén, for example. There is also a series of package trips, *trenes turisticos*, which include accommodation in very good Andalusian hotels and sightseeing tours. You can book these trips from abroad through IBER-RAIL, C/ Capitán Haya 55, Madrid, tel: 912793605 or 913793200.

Intercity Buses
Smaller towns and large cities in Spain are linked for the most part by buses. Information is available from travel agents or from the bus companies. In smaller towns buses depart from the main square, with schedules available in the bar or store in closest proximity to the square.

PRACTICAL TIPS FROM A TO Z

Accommodation
This travel guide contains only a small selection of the huge choice of accommodations available. For the larger towns we

have recommended accommodation in all available categories. We have tried to choose centrally situated and architecturally attractive accommodations. City tourist offices do not generally arrange accommodations or reservations.

The following categories for lodging exist in Spain:

H . . . . Hotel
HR. . . . . Hotel Residencia (holiday hotel for longer stays)
HA. . . . . Hotel Apartamentos
RA . . . . . Residencia Apartamentos
M . . . . Motel
Hs. . . . . Hostal (simple hotel)
P . . . . Pension (in cities often long-stay accomodation)
HsR . . . . Hostal Residencia (often long-stay accomodation)
F . . . . Fonda (the most simple type of guest house)

The hotel categories shown in the INFO sections of the travel chapters in this book correspond to the following price ranges:
●●● starting at 16,000 pesetas; ●● 8,000 to 16,000 pesetas; ● up to 8,000 pesetas. All hotels, regardless of category, are usually clean, but the beds are sometimes bad, even in the very good hotels. Noise is no cause for complaint.

Paradores Nacionales are state-run hotels in the upper price brackets and almost always in a nice setting. Illustrated catalogs can be obtained from any tourist office. In the high season book ahead, which you can do from abroad. Central reservations for *Paradores Nacionales* in Spain: C/ Requena 3, 28013 Madrid, tel. 915166666.

Breakdown and Accident Services

The Royal Automobile Club, RACE, helps in the event of a breakdown or accident. It has agreements with the following foreign automobile clubs: ADAC, DTC, AvD, AA, RAC, ACI and TCI. The national emergency towing service can be reached in Madrid at tel. 915933333. If the police are to be notified, contact the *Policia Municipal* within a city, and the *Guardia Civil de Traffico* if outside a city.

Car Rental

The easiest way to rent a car is by credit card: without one you will be asked to leave a deposit of around US $850. You will need to show your passport and a drivers license which is more than one year old. There are often special rates on weekends.

Cinemas

There are some cinemas in bigger cities which show foreign films in their original version (*versión original*) or with subtitles (*versión subtitulada*).

Electricity

The voltage in Spain is 220 volts and 50 Hz. Most hotels have standard European plug sockets, but if not you can buy an adapter in any electrical shop.

Etiquette

Although Spain is part of Europe, Northern Europeans and North Americans will find that some modes of behavior are different from what they are used to. There is a polite form of address (*usted*), but most people use the informal *tú* in shops and restaurants. In many restaurants and cafés it is considered normal to throw rubbish on the floor – the places are swept often enough to maintain hygiene. Central European customs of speaking more quietly after 10 at night or turning down televisions and stereos are unknown in Spain.

Festivals

Every town has a local fiesta once or twice a year which can last for anything from a long weekend to two weeks. Visitors will have to put up with more noise, especially at nighttime. Complaints will only meet with a lack of understanding. The only thing to do is join in!

Gas Stations
Credit cards are accepted at all tollway service stations. These are open 24 hours a day, whereas other gas stations tend to close at around 8 p.m.

Golf
Golf courses can be found especially along the Mediterranean coast. Those who wish to golf in Spain must be members of a golfing association. A list of golf courses is available from tourist offices.

Guides
Spanish tour guides have to study for three years and are usually well-qualified. In most towns you can book English, French or German guides through the tourist office.

Holidays
National holidays are: January I (New Year's Day); January 6 (Epiphany); Easter (Maundy Thursday, Good Friday and Easter Monday); May 1 (International Workers Day); August 15 (Assumption Day); October 12 (Virgen del Pilar and Columbus Day); November 1 (All Saints' Day); December 6 (Constitution Day); December 8 (Day of the Immaculate Conception); December 25 (Christmas Day).

In addition, each region and every town also has its own local holidays.

Meal Times
The day begins slowly and comparatively late in Spain. You have breakfast in a bar with a coffee and something to dunk in it, preferably *churros* (fritters). In Spain the main meal of the day is eaten between 2 and 4 p.m. At lunchtime cheaper meals are offered in most restaurants and cafés. Almost all of them have a good lunch menu which includes bread and wine. At small inobtrusive places – with low prices and the menu jotted down on a piece of paper – you can be sure to find simple but delicious home cooking.

The main Spanish news program is broadcast at 3 p.m., and after that it's siesta time until 5 p.m. Dinnertime begins at 9 p.m. in restaurants, and bedtime, especially in summer, is not before 1 a.m., even for children.

Museums / Art Galleries
Private art galleries have the same opening times as shops, but some open on Sundays, too. Public museums and galleries are almost always closed on Sunday afternoon and Monday. There is often a day during the week when admission for EU nationals is free.

Opening Times
Shops usually open between 9 and 10 in the morning and have a break between 2 and 5 p.m., which might be half an hour earlier in the winter and in the north. In the evenings they close around 8 p.m. Shops are open on Saturdays, sometimes in the afternoon, too. Department stores and shops in the city centers are generally open throughout the day and close a little later in the evenings. Museums and sights usually have the same opening hours as businesses, though they are often open on Sundays only in the morning and are closed Mondays.

Opening times may vary somewhat from year to year and are considerably longer in summer than in winter. Sights outside the towns are often closed completely outside the high season. You can always ask for the caretaker to unlock the door on village churches for a look inside.

Pharmacies
Farmácias can be found everywhere. They are well stocked and sell many medicines without prescriptions. Opening times are as for shops.

Photography
You are allowed to take photos at most monuments and in most churches and museums, but often video cameras are

Guidelines

prohibited. Flash bulbs are almost always forbidden.

Postal Services

The post offices (*correos*) are often open in the mornings only, but you can buy stamps in every *estanco,* the state tobacco shops. Letters and postcards to EU countries cost the same. National inland rates are different for local and long-distance letters.

Press

In cities and holiday resorts on the Mediterranean there is always a good selection of international daily newspapers available in addition to the national ones. Spanish newspapers are also printed on Sundays.

Restaurants

Most restaurants offer inexpensive set menus for lunch, including bread, wine or beer and dessert. Especially good meals can often be found in the cheapest and least pretentious eateries.

Rules of the Road

The speed limit for cars and motorcycles within city limits is 50 kmh, on highways 100 kmh, and on freeways and toll highways 120 kmh.

Passing is forbidden within 100 meters of the crest of a hill, as well as on stretches of road with less than 200 meters visibility.

Using private vehicles to tow cars is not allowed.

Using a portable phone in a car is only allowed if it has a "hands off "feature, i.e., if you keep both hands on the wheel.

Special street signs: *Alto* = Stop; *Atención, Cuidado* = Attention, Caution; *Viraje Peligroso* = Dangerous Curve; *Ceda el Paso* = Yield Right of Way; *Paso Prohibido* = Do Not Enter; *Prohibido Aparcar* = No Parking.

The blood alcohol limit for drivers is 0.5 ppm.

Telecommunications

If you make a call to Spain from abroad, you have to dial the complete area code with the number; this also applies to calls made within Spain – even local calls. The country code for Spain is +34. You can make international calls from all public telephones. Dial 07 for the international network and wait for the tone. Then dial the country code (England 44; Canada and the US 1; Ireland 353; New Zealand 64; Australia 61).

Dial 003 for national information, 008 for European information, and 005 for information for the rest of the world. In most towns there are offices of the telephone company *Telefónica* with long distance phone booths in the *locutorio*. There are now many private *locutorios* which are generally much cheaper than the phone company. Cards for public telephones can be purchased in any *estanco* (tobacco shop). Coin phones take 25, 50 and 100 peseta coins.

Theft

Even a well-disguised tourist is obviously a tourist. In cities, never carry a handbag on the streets, keep your wallet in your trouser pocket, or better yet, in a money belt worn under your clothes. The busier the pavement, the surer you can be that someone will be trying to snatch someone else's purse or pick someone's pocket. Your passport, tickets, travelers checks, etc. are safer locked in your suitcase in the hotel or in the hotel safe than on your person.

Foreign cars are predestined to be broken into, especially if anything can be seen inside. Usually the small window on the pavement side is smashed with a stone. Under no circumstances should valuable papers be kept in your glove compartment! You cannot safely leave a car with a radio on any Spanish street. Guarded underground garages take no responsibility for the contents of your car, but offer certain protection.

If important documents are stolen, their replacement will be facilitated if you have kept a written record of the document's number, and place and date of issue. The smartest thing to do would be to make photocopies of all your important documents and keep them separate from the originals.

Time

Although geographically Spain lies in another time zone, it follows Central European time. Because the country lies so far west, it stays light much later in summer. The Canary Islands are one hour behind the rest of the country.

Tipping

In cafés and restaurants tips are usually included in the price. The additional sum on the bill is *IVA*, value added tax. Tips are still welcomed, of course. It is not advisable to offer traffic police or Guardia Civil a "tip" in order to try to get them to change their minds about issuing a ticket.

Tourist Information

In every provincial capital and in many tourist centers there are tourist information offices (i = *Información,* or *Oficina de Turismo)* which will provide you with printed information and maps. They follow normal opening times. Only in the more important tourist areas are they open on Sunday mornings in summer. There are also *Comunidades Autónomas* offices in some towns.

Weights and Measures

Weights, measures and clothing sizes are the same as in other continental European countries.

ADDRESSES

Spanish Tourist Offices Abroad

AUSTRALIA: 203 Castlereagh Street, Suite 21, Sidney, NSW 2000, tel. (612) 264-7966.

CANADA: 2 Bloor Street West, 34th Floor, Toronto, Ontario M4W 3E2, tel. (416) 961-3131.
UK: 22-23 Manchester Square, London W1M 5AP, tel. (207) 486-8077.
US: 845 N. Michigan Ave., Suite 915E, Chicago, IL 60611, tel. (312) 642-1992; San Vicente Plaza Bldg., 8383 Wilshire Blvd., Suite 956, Beverly Hills, CA 90211, tel. (213) 658-7188; 1221 Brickell Ave., Miami, FL 33131, tel. (305) 358-1992; 666 Fifth Ave., 35th Floor, New York, NY 10103, tel. (212) 265-8822.

Spanish Embassies Abroad

AUSTRALIA: 15 Arkana St., Yarralumla, P.O. Box 9076 Deakin, ACT 2600, Canberra, tel. 733555.
CANADA: 350 Spark St., Suite 802, Ottowa, Ontario, tel. 237-2193.
IRELAND: 17A Merlyn Park, Ballsbridge, Dublin 4, tel. 269-1640.
UK: 39 Chesham Place, London SW1X 8SB, tel. 235-5555.
US: 2375 Pennsylvania Ave. NW, Washington, D.C. 20037, tel. (202) 452-0100.

SPANISH STYLISTICS

Alcazaba (Arabic: al-kasbah): Fortified district; citadel.
Alcázar (Arabic: al-kasr = fortress): Residence or palace of a Moorish ruler.
Azulejo: Colorful glazed tiles of kiln-fired clay.
Visigótico: West Gothic (Visigoth), late classical period (5th-6th century).
Muqarnas: Honeycomb ceiling ornamentation of plaster. Common in Islamic countries from the 11th century on.
Asturiano: The Pre-Romanesque in Asturias, which developed without Moorish influence (9th century).
Mozárabe: Mozarabic; the architectural style of the Christians who migrated from the Moorish-occupied regions of the south to the liberated northern regions.
Mudéjar: Style of the Arabian master builders who worked for Christians after the *Reconquista* (14th century).

Moriscos: Moslem converts to Christianity.

Isabelino: Late-Gothic variation of Renaissance; the predominant style during the reign of Isabella I (15th century).

Plateresco: Decorative style of the early Renaissance (16th century).

Herreriano: Strict Renaissance style named for Juan de Herrera, Philip II's architect (16th century).

Hispano-Flamenco: Architectural style under the Habsburgs with Flemish influences.

Churrigueresco: Late-Baroque sytle of the Churrigueras (I 7th century).

THE LANGUAGES OF SPAIN

In Spain, the Romantic languages of *Catalá* and *Gallego* are spoken in addition to *Castillano,* or proper Spanish. Some of the populace of the Basque Country and Navarra speak the very unique Basque language, which cannot be tied to any other language group.

Special pronunciations of Castilian Spanish: ll is pronounced like 'y' in yes; c before e or i like 'th', otherwise like 'k'; qu before i and e like 'k'; v like soft 'b'; z before a vowel or at the end of a word like 'th', otherwise like 's'; ñ like 'ny' as in canyon; j like a throaty 'h'; h is always silent.

GLOSSARY

Good morning	*buenos días*
(after 2 p.m.)	*buenas tardes*
Good night	*buenas noches*
Hello	*hola*
Please	*por favor*
Thank you	*gracias*
Yes	*Sí*
No	*no*
Goodbye	*adiós*
Excuse me	*perdón*
How are you?	*¿Que tal?*
Good	*bién/bueno*
What time is it?	*¿Qué hora es?*

How much is it?	*¿Cuánto cuesta ésto?*
Where is...?	*¿Dónde está... ?*
to the right	*a la derecha*
to the left	*a la izquierda*

Numbers:

one	*uno, un, una*
two	*dos*
three	*tres*
four	*cuatro*
five	*cinco*
six	*seis*
seven	*siete*
eight	*ocho*
nine	*nueve*
ten	*diez*
eleven	*once*
twelve	*doce*
twenty	*veinte*
hundred	*cien, ciento*
thousand	*mil*

Time:

today	*hoy*
tomorrow	*mañana*
yesterday	*ayer*
minute	*minuto*
hour	*hora*
day	*día*
week	*semana*
month	*mes*
year	*año*

Days of the week:

Monday	*Lunes*
Tuesday	*Martes*
Wednesday	*Miércoles*
Thursday	*Jueves*
Friday	*Viernes*
Saturday	*Sábado*
Sunday	*Domingo*
Holiday	*Festivo*

Asking for a room:

Do you have a room?	*¿Hay habitación libre?*
double room	*habitación doble*
single room	*habitación sencilla*
with breakfast	*con desayuno*
quiet	*tranquilo*

In a restaurant:

menu of the day	*menú del día*
dessert	*postre*

bread . . . . *pan*
drink . . . . *bebida*
wine . . . . *vino*
beer . . . . *cerveza*
mineral water . . . . *agua mineral*
carbonated/uncarbonated . . *con/sin gas*
espresso . . . . *café solo*
espresso with milk . . . . . *café cortado*
milk coffee . . . . *café con leche*
tea . . . . *té*
tea with lemon . . . . *té con limón*
breakfast . . . . *desayuno*
omelette . . . . *tortilla*
eggs . . . . *huevos*
potato omelette . . . . *tortilla española*
fish . . . . *pescado*
soup . . . . *sopa*
meat . . . . *carne*
beef . . . . *carne de vaca*
pork . . . . *cerdo*
veal . . . . *ternera*
chicken . . . . *pollo*
lamb . . . . *cordero*
fried . . . . *frito*
grilled . . . . *a la plancha*
roast . . . . *asado*
in batter . . . . *rebozada*
salad . . . . *ensalada*
vegetables . . . . *legumbres*
green vegetables . . . . *verduras*
The bill please! . *¡La cuenta, por favor!*
Seafood:

sea pike . . . . *merluza*
trout . . . . *trucha*
salmon . . . . *salmón*
tuna . . . . *atún*
swordfish . . . . *pez espada*
squid . . . . *calamares*
octopus . . . . *pulpo*
mussels . . . . *mejillones*
shrimp . . . . *gambas*

AUTHORS

Gabriel Calvo Lopez-Guerrero is a professor of language and literature, a journalist and an author of screenplays. Today he lives and writes in Madrid. He penned the "Fiestas" feature.

Mercedes de la Cruz is a professor of literature and "flamencologist." She wrote the feature "Flamenco."

Marion Golder is a professor of literature and study tour leader. Since studying in Granada she has become an expert on Andalusia.

Elke Homburg studied literature, theater and philosophy. She has been traveling to Spain for many years as a study tour leader. A freelance author and journalist, she has written several books on the Iberian Peninsula. For this book she wrote the feature "From Kitchen and Wine Cellar."

Dr. Sabine Tzschaschel studied Spain, Latin America and the European Union while at university. She currently lives in Leipzig. She wrote the feature "Sherry."

PHOTOGRAPHERS

Guidelines

Explore the World

NELLES MAPS

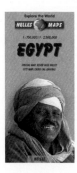

AVAILABLE TITELS

Afghanistan 1 : 1 500 000
Argentina *(Northern)*, **Uruguay**
1 : 2 500 000
Argentina *(Southern)*, **Uruguay**
1 : 2 500 000
Australia 1 : 4 000 000
Bangkok - *and Greater Bangkok*
1 : 75 000 / 1 : 15 000
Burma → *Myanmar*
Caribbean - **Bermuda, Bahamas,
Greater Antilles** 1 : 2 500 000
Caribbean - **Lesser Antilles**
1 : 2 500 000
Central America 1 : 1 750 000
Central Asia 1 : 1 750 000
China - *Northeastern*
1 : 1 500 000
China - *Northern* 1 : 1 500 000
China - *Central* 1 : 1 500 000
China - *Southern* 1 : 1 500 000
Colombia - **Ecuador** 1 : 2 500 000
Crete - Kreta 1 : 200 000
Dominican Republic - Haiti
1 : 600 000
Egypt 1 : 2 500 000 / 1 : 750 000
Hawaiian Islands
1 : 330 000 / 1 : 125 000
Hawaiian Islands – **Kaua'i**
1 : 150 000 / 1 : 35 000
Hawaiian Islands – **Honolulu**

- O'ahu 1 : 35 000 / 1 : 150 000
Hawaiian Islands – **Maui -
Moloka'i**
- **Lāna'i** 1 : 150 000 / 1 : 35 000
Hawaiian Islands – **Hawai'i, The
Big
Island** 1 : 330 000 / 1 : 125 000
Himalaya 1 : 1 500 000
Hong Kong 1 : 22 500
Indian Subcontinent 1 : 4 000 000
India - *Northern* 1 : 1 500 000
India - *Western* 1 : 1 500 000
India - *Eastern* 1 : 1 500 000
India - *Southern* 1 : 1 500 000
India - *Northeastern - Bangladesh*
1 : 1 500 000
Indonesia 1 : 4 000 000
Indonesia **Sumatra** 1 : 1 500 000
Indonesia **Java - Nusa Tenggara**
1 : 1 500 000
Indonesia **Bali - Lombok**
1 : 180 000
Indonesia **Kalimantan**
1 : 1 500 000
Indonesia **Java - Bali** 1 : 650 000
Indonesia **Sulawesi** 1 : 1 500 000
Indonesia **Irian Jaya - Maluku**
1 : 1 500 000
Jakarta 1 : 22 500
Japan 1 : 1 500 000
Kenya 1 : 1 100 000
Korea 1 : 1 500 000

Malaysia 1 : 1 500 000
West Malaysia 1 : 650 000
Manila 1 : 17 500
Mexico 1 : 2 500 000
Myanmar (Burma) 1 : 1 500 000
Nepal 1 : 500 000 / 1 : 1 500 000
Nepal Trekking **Khumbu Himal -
Solu Khumbu** 1 : 75 000
New Zealand 1 : 1 250 000
Pakistan 1 : 1 500 000
Peru - Ecuador 1 : 2 500 000
Philippines 1 : 1 500 000
Singapore 1 : 22 500
Southeast Asia 1 : 4 000 000
South Pacific Islands
1 : 13 000 000
Sri Lanka 1 : 450 000
Taiwan 1 : 400 000
Tanzania - Rwanda, Burundi
1 : 1 500 000
Thailand 1 : 1 500 000
Uganda 1 : 700 000
Venezuela - Guyana, Suriname,
French Guiana 1 : 2 500 000
Vietnam, Laos, Cambodia
1 : 1 500 000

FORTHCOMING

Bolivia, **Paraguay** 1 : 2 500 000
Chile 1 : 2 500 000
Cuba 1 : 775 000

*Nelles Maps are top quality cartography!
Relief mapping, kilometer charts and tourist attractions.
Always up-to-date!*